PRAISE

THE KING OF HOPE

The words of Dan Carroll consistently bring life and hope to thousands. He has become a gift to this generation—a comforter, a wise friend, a spiritual father.

John Dawson
President, Youth With a Mission International

I am rejoiced by every feature of Dan Carroll's life—his marriage and family, his pastoral leadership and his global vision for evangelism. The appearance of his new book, *The King of Hope*, is an opportunity for multitudes to discover the enriching, practical and thoroughly biblical communication that characterizes his gracious and edifying style. In these times in which many have become weary with the superficial and artificial—often pedaled as inspirational truth—Dan's writing cuts to the core of "the real" and points the way with a shepherd's touch to the God-intended "reality" of answers and guidelines for life. It will lift hearts, focus vision, bring wisdom and grow people forward in God's intended blessings for their lives.

Dr. Jack W. Hayford
Chancellor, The King's University, Dallas/Los Angeles

In an age in which the word *mega* is often used to describe or imply success in the contemporary church, God has raised up a Dan Carroll. Pastor Dan has a heart for the grassroots needs of everyday people! God has given him an unusual anointing to walk in the likeness of the Master, whose message was directed to ordinary people. Dan Carroll is an incarnation of the mandate to go into the world with a message that crosses ethnic, cultural and geographic boundaries. He is on a mission from God to make disciples and to touch and change lives for the kingdom of our Lord. Pastor Dan is committed to equipping the church to do the work of ministry in an ever-changing contemporary culture.

Dr. Kenneth C. Ulmer
Board of Trustees, The King's University

THE KING OF HOPE

T H E
KING OF HOPE

FINDING YOUR STORY
IN THE CHRISTMAS STORY

O O O

DAN CARROLL

Published by Water of Life Community Church
Fontana, California, U.S.A.
www.wateroflifecc.org
Printed in the U.S.A.

Cover design by Ryan DePaola
Interior design by Rob Williams

ISBN 978-0-9913138-0-8

Rights for publishing this book outside the U.S.A. or in non-English languages are
administered by Water of Life Community Church. For additional information
please visit www.wateroflifecc.org, e-mail info@wateroflifecc.org or
kingofhopebook@wateroflifecc.org or write to Water of Life Community Church,
7625 East Avenue, Fontana, CA 92336, U.S.A.

To order copies of this book in bulk quantities,
please e-mail kingofhopebook@wateroflifecc.org.

CONTENTS

Preface 9

Introduction: A Christmas Carroll 11

CHAPTER 1 POP QUIZ: THE REAL CHRISTMAS STORY 15

1. Christmas: A Story of Hope 19

CHAPTER 2 POP QUIZ: JOSEPH AND MARY 35

2. Pressing Through to Hope 39

CHAPTER 3 POP QUIZ: THE SHEPHERDS 63

3. Obeying the Word of Hope 65

CHAPTER 4 POP QUIZ: THE WISE MEN 83

4. Finding Hope in Hard Times 87

5. The King of Hope in You 107

About the Author 131

About Water of Life 133

Our Core Values 135

○ ○ ○ PREFACE ○ ○ ○

This little book has been compiled mostly from messages that I preached during a recent Christmas season. Christmas is a season that should provoke hope in us, but oftentimes it brings forth a sense of despair—despair of life, of relationships lost, of dreams dashed and of wounds that don't seem to heal. Rather than living in anticipation of the joy and life that the newborn Savior can bring, many shrink away during the Christmas season into protective armor, just hoping to survive the holiday weeks one more time. That, my friend, is not God's heart for you. Our God is the God of the desperate and the despairing. He sent His Son into a world filled with pressure and pain, oppression and heartache. He is very familiar with you and your situation, and He has come to impart hope and life to you.

You may know God intimately, or you may not know Him at all. But I am certain of this: you need His hope in your journey. What really matters is that *God knows you*, and He has come to touch your situation with His hope. But receiving God's hope is only possible when you bow down, humble your heart and yield your will to Him and ask Him to have His way in you, in your situation, in your pain and in your disappointment. It is then and only then that God's Spirit is loosed to touch you, to impart hope to you and to begin to put life back into you where you have been robbed.

As you read, please remember that the Christmas story is really your story. From Joseph and Mary to the shepherds in the field to the wise men who traveled so far, this is your journey and mine. This book was written to impart hope to people who are battling with real life and real struggles. Open your heart to God's hand touching your circumstances, and see if His hope doesn't once again rise up in you.

Pastor Dan
November 2013, Fontana, California

○ ○ ○ A CHRISTMAS CARROLL ○ ○ ○

We all look forward to Christmas. It's the one time of the year when we count down to the big day. We anticipate the celebration for weeks, even months. Nowadays it seems as if the Christmas season starts earlier and earlier.

It's crazy, isn't it, the frenzy we build up. We rush around to buy presents, select trees and erect mangers on our front lawns. We sing carols, wear zany red hats and wonder what Aunt Lucy got for us that is in that big blue box under the tree.

Wow, kids can really build up their expectations. Sometimes it's nearly impossible for them to go to sleep on Christmas Eve. Have you ever been there? I have! Maybe as a child you just had to know what you were getting, and you snuck a peek in advance. Perhaps you shook a package and guessed what was inside. Or maybe you gingerly untied the pretty bow, slid off the ribbon and secretly opened a present early—and then quickly rewrapped it, hoping that no one would notice. *Now I'm sure none of you has ever done that! Right?*

I was raised in a middle-class home in the suburbs. There were just four of us. Dad worked hard at his blue-collar job. Mom was a homebody who always took care of our needs and made a family dinner for us every night. Jeanine, my older sister, was as nice as

I was ornery. She was the smartest person in her class, which left me always trying to keep up. Life wasn't ideal, but we were happy. We had a simple life and, compared to many, a good one.

The Carroll family always celebrated Christmas. Dad and Mom would pick out the tree, and Jeanine and I would help put on the lights. Mom would make cookies and other treats for us. Funny how those simple moments seem so precious today. Christmas was like life—simple yet always full of expectation.

Jeanine and I knew that we would always have something nice waiting for us under the tree, but we were never overwhelmed by expensive gifts. Oftentimes Dad would find a discarded bike or piece of furniture and rebuild it, transforming it into a beautiful present for one of us kids. Some people might feel embarrassed at the idea that their father would salvage a used object, fix it up and then give it to them for Christmas. I get it, but that thought never entered our minds. Our father's care and his desire to provide for us always prevailed. We were grateful.

One of my favorite Christmas memories involves a red bike. I had a paper route in those days, but my little Sting-Ray bike wasn't really up to the task. For months I had jabbered away about how I needed a bigger bike, but I never thought that I would actually get one. As Christmas approached that year, I knew something was up. At night my dad would disappear into the garage for hours. When he was finished working each night, he would lock the garage door so that we couldn't peek inside, and then he would return to the house without saying a word. I guessed that he might be creating some kind of present—maybe a desk for Jeanine—but I never imagined that he might be overhauling a bike for me. Boy, was I surprised come Christmas morning. Dad wheeled in my present:

a big, heavy-duty red bicycle. It was perfect for me. Yes, it was used (I mean *pre-owned*), but it was exactly what I needed.

This is how God worked at the first Christmas, isn't it? He sent Jesus to a trough that was pre-owned—we call it a manger, but it was actually a feeding trough! When the prophets of old predicted the coming of the King of the universe, the hope of mankind, this surely is not what they envisioned. But God knew what we needed. We didn't need more glitz; we needed more heart. My heavenly Father's heart, like my earthly father's, broke through to us at Christmas. The gift of His Son is all that we really need.

I raised my children with a small Christmas tradition that reminds us of God's heart for us. In the Carroll house, we opened no gifts until we had read the Christmas story together as a family. That drove our kids mad when they were little, but over the years the Father's heart grabbed their hearts too, and He built a tradition for all of us that is followed to this day in our home. The size or number of the gifts doesn't matter to us as much as the heart of the giver. Ultimately, our family can give in this way because we know the King of hope. As we read the Christmas story each year in our home, each of us discovers his or her own story anew.

In this book let me introduce you to the reality of Christmas and to why it means hope for you, me and everyone everywhere. As you read, if you look, I believe that you will find your story in the Christmas story.

THE REAL CHRISTMAS STORY

We are about to look at the true story of Christmas. A story of hope. Do you need hope?

Hope is crucial to our wellbeing. But before we dive into the story of Christmas and all that it offers, we have some issues to clear up about the events surrounding the first Christmas.

You probably know about the shepherds, how they were out in the field and had a visitation from some angels. Then, the Bible tells us, they decided to go "see this thing" (Luke 2:15) that they had been told about. Well, it wasn't a "thing," was it? It was a baby. Don't ever go to the hospital and tell a lady that you want to see the "thing" she's just given birth to. She'll slap you in the head, right? The shepherds didn't look for a thing. They looked for a King. We'll talk about what "thing" means later.

And the King was likely born in a cave. In Bethlehem there are large caves, big, swooping caverns, and in Jesus' day people would build an inn in front of a cave. The cave would become a built-in stable or barn for the inn. So it is likely that Jesus was born not in the building in front but in the cave at the back of the inn.

One Christmas after I had preached about this, a family e-mailed me a picture of their nativity scene. They had moved

Joseph and Mary and the shepherds and animals and wise men into their fireplace because they thought it would be more biblical that way—the scene would look like it was in a cave. "Okay," I told them, "that's a good start, but you still have a problem. You've got the wise guys in there." The wise men weren't at the manger scene. So I told them, "Look, you need to move those guys to the other end of the house, because they're still on their way to Bethlehem. They haven't gotten to the baby yet."

That e-mail provoked me to think that a Christmas quiz would be a good idea. So here is your first pop quiz (you'll find the rest of them as you go through the book). The first time I asked these questions at my church, nobody got them all right, so the challenge is on. Here we go:

1. The baby Jesus was born in

    a. A car
    b. A manger
    c. A hurry
    d. A barn
    e. Who knows?!

2. What animals were present at Jesus' birth?

    a. Cows, sheep and camels
    b. Cows, sheep and donkeys
    c. Lions, tigers and bears
    d. None of the above

3. What is a manger anyway?

    a. A barn
    b. A place for hay
    c. A feeding trough
    d. A Greek term for a church nursery

4. When did the baby Jesus cry?

    a. When He opened the wise men's gifts
    b. Whenever babies usually cried
    c. When the cattle started lowing
    d. No crying He makes

5. In what books of the Bible will you find these fascinating facts?

    a. Matthew, Mark, Luke and John
    b. Matthew and Luke
    c. Mark and Matthew
    d. Matthew, Mark and Luke

Okay, here are your answers. How do you think you did? Let's take a look.

Number 1. The baby Jesus was born in what? Who knows? We don't know the exact details about His birth. But *after* His birth He was laid in what? A manger.

Number 2. What animals were present? The Bible never mentions any animals being present.

Number 3. What's a manger? A feeding trough.

Number 4. When did baby Jesus cry? He cried whenever babies usually cried, because Jesus was fully human and fully God. Isn't that right?

Number 5. In what books of the Bible can you find these fascinating facts? You can find them in the Gospels of Matthew and Luke.

When I asked in the second service how many people had gotten all the answers right, two hands were raised, so that was better—but one of the people who raised her hand had been in the previous service!

How many did you get right?

Chapter 1

CHRISTMAS: A STORY OF HOPE

*Today in the city of David there has been born for you
a Savior, who is Christ the Lord.*

LUKE 2:11

I love Christmas. Christmas rocks!

"But Pastor Dan, Jesus wasn't really born on December 25!"

I know that.

"Pastor Dan, we don't even like Christmas anymore. It's become a made-for-TV event. It's all commercialized."

I know that too. I've heard all the complaints. But Christmas was God's idea.

All of us are glad that there are holidays like Christmas. Right? But what is a holiday? It's a holy day. The word *holiday* comes from the twelfth-century English word *haligdaeg*. *Halig* means "holy," and *daeg* means "day." Originally, a holiday was a day set apart for the purpose of celebrating or commemorating a religious event in history. It was a day originated by God, a holy day.

Holidays are also meant to give us rest. That is one reason God put the festivals in the Israelites' lives—they needed breaks!

Don't we all? What if we never had a holiday? We would be bored with the never-ending, day-after-day drudgery of our work. We would be exhausted too. The human body cannot handle nonstop work. Thankfully, God knows our physical limits. After all, He created us. In fact, on the seventh day of creation—after Adam and Eve had been created—He instituted a day of rest.

Today we have Christmas, Thanksgiving, Easter and all sorts of festivals and holidays. Each of them is intended to bless us and to bring us life, some physically and some spiritually.

But what does Christmas mean? What is this holiday really all about?

Christmas ushered in a King. We all know what a king is, of course. A king is the supreme ruler over a nation or territory, and he generally rules for life. A king is not like a president. The people don't vote him in, and they don't get to overturn his decrees in a parliamentary body. The king is established by right of heredity. He is born to his position. And what the king says goes! A selfish king might take advantage of his authority to oppress people, but a good king can use his position to bless and shepherd those in his care. I think I'd prefer a good king, wouldn't you?

A kingdom is whatever the king has rule or lordship over.

When a king comes into power, he gets busy right away establishing his kingdom, right? A kingdom is whatever the king has rule or lordship over. For most kings establishing a kingdom means building a military, levying taxes, regulating the economy, and generally establishing his rule over the peoples and lands within his sphere of government.

Christmas ushered in a King. But the kingdom Jesus established didn't look like any other king's. Jesus didn't go around recruiting military leaders and getting ready to take over the Roman world. No. He established His kingdom in people's lives.

Simply put, Jesus' kingdom was that which He was Lord over and had rule over—people's hearts. He taught people about things like repentance and forgiveness and healing and hope and love, and then He invited people to enter into His kingdom through faith and obedience. People often didn't know what to make of this unconventional King who got into people's personal business and asked them to let Him be Lord over such things as their finances, their emotions and their time.

Jesus' coming to earth was all about breaking into each of our worlds and showing us our need of a King who could give us real answers for our real problems. Christmas ushered in a King who would give life and hope to those who didn't have any and who would fulfill God's destiny in each of our lives.

The Bible talks about three things that are crucial to our well-being: faith, hope and love. They're all important. And we talk about faith and love all the time. *But what about hope?* We don't hear about that one as often. But the fact is, my friend, that we live and die on hope. Humans must have hope, or we won't live. That's reality.

Did you know that Christmas is full of hope? It provides an awesome amount of expectation. We see that when we celebrate every year. We buy gifts for our kids, and we wrap them and put them under the tree, and our kids go crazy with excitement and anticipation.

The hope of Christmas is not an accident. It's part of our destiny. Let's look at Luke chapter 2. This is the Christmas story:

> While they were [in Bethlehem], the days were completed for [Mary] to give birth. And she gave birth to her firstborn son; and she wrapped Him in cloths, and laid Him in a manger, because there was no room for them in the inn. . . . "Today in the city of David there has been born for you a Savior, who is Christ the Lord." (2:6-7, 11)

This is an amazing, life-giving story, but some of us have read it so many times that we don't even get it anymore! "Pastor Dan," you say, "we already know this story. We see Joseph and Mary and the baby every Christmas on people's front lawns."

Yes, but look a little closer. That title, the term *Christ*, literally means "the reigning, ruling One." It means that God gave us a king at Christmas—a king who wants to rule over each of our worlds and give us hope and possibility that we can't get anywhere else. That is cause for anticipation and expectation and hope on our part.

Before we dive further into the Christmas story, let's look back to the Old Testament at another story of hope. Do you remember the story of Joseph? He was the eleventh of Jacob's twelve sons, and the favorite of his father. But despite being his dad's favorite—or maybe because of it—Joseph's life was brutal. His brothers were jealous of him. In their hatred they threw him in a pit and then sold him into slavery, and at seventeen years of age, Joseph ended up in Egypt, a slave in Potiphar's house. I know. You're wondering, *where's the hope in this story?*

The interesting thing about Joseph is that everywhere the guy landed, he rose to the top. Everywhere. The Bible says that in no time Joseph was running all the other servants in Potiphar's house.

Some of you might think that sounds pretty great. "Yeah, he got a rough deal from his brothers, but now he's not doing too badly." Let me explain Potiphar. He was the chief executioner in Egypt. If one of his servants made a mistake with him, he didn't reprove him—he just cut his head off. This is who Joseph worked for. But here's another interesting thing about Joseph: he didn't live in fear in his service every day to Potiphar; he lived in faith. That's why he rose to the top. He didn't live in his circumstances and in the pain of having been rejected by his brothers. No, he made a decision: "I'm not going to let what's happened stop me."

The hope of Christmas is not an accident.
It's part of our destiny.

And then, when things were going fairly well for Joseph, Potiphar's wife hit on him. Joseph told her no, and she didn't like that too well. She ran to her husband and accused Joseph of hitting on *her*, and the poor guy was unjustly thrown into jail! He ended up in jail for doing the right thing. Would you be angry about that? Would you be bitter? The amazing thing about Joseph is that he wasn't.

23

So the guy ended up in jail—and in no time he was running the whole place. He rose to the top again. Why? Because the Lord was with him. And why was the Lord with him? Because Joseph believed God. He believed beyond his circumstances.

You see, back when he'd been at home, enjoying his favored-son status, God had spoken into Joseph's life. God had given him a couple of dreams, and in them He had given Joseph a glimpse of his future. Joseph probably didn't fully understand the dreams when he was first given them, but he sensed that God was speaking destiny over his life. Now, stuck in an Egyptian prison, far from his family, his home, his country, Joseph held onto the promises of God. He refused to let go of the fact that God was good and that God would fulfill His purpose in his life (see Gen. 37, 39).

Had Joseph's circumstances knocked him down over and over and over? Yes. But remember, Jesus told us that in this world we would have troubles (see John 16:33). He didn't pull any punches; life is hard. But here's the thing: our tribulations create perseverance. That's what Romans 5:1-5 teaches us. Our trials create perseverance, and perseverance creates proven character. And what does proven character produce? Hope.

Have you noticed that we're a little short on proven character these days? We don't have it anymore, because people don't stay put in the trial. Nobody holds steady in the pain. We all say, "Man, I can't live with this. It's so bad, I've just got to get some drugs. I've got to get some food. I've got to get some sex. I've got to get outta here!" Joseph said, "No, I'll stay here, because God's bigger than this. He'll take me past it."

I mean, the guy could have reasoned differently. He could have said, "Look, Potiphar's wife, she's kind of a knockout. If I have sex

with her, man, I deserve it. I've lost my family, my freedom, everything familiar to me." But he didn't do that. He honored God.
And he was thrown into prison. Joseph probably ended up being
in prison for ten years. Ten years is a long time to keep believing,
especially when you're in jail. Especially when you're in jail unfair-
ly! But Joseph kept believing.

No one can do that without hope.

A little girl walked up to me one night after I finished preaching and handed me a letter. Here's what it said:

Dear Pastor Dan,

I listen to your sermons a lot. I've been through a lot
of stuff. I was put in foster care for five years in five different foster homes. One year I was in a group home. I was
taken away because of drugs. I've been abused. My sisters
got split up and put in different homes. My little sister
stayed with me. She was about one year old, and I was
eight at the time. My older sister got put in a foster home
as well. My other sister was put in juvenile hall. My mom
went to jail. My mom split up with my dad, and we lived
in Las Vegas, and I was four. My mom moved to California with my sisters and I, but I was taken away again, me
and my sister. We went to another city to a foster home.
We stayed there for a year and a half. The family ended up
moving to Mexico, so they moved us to another place in a
small town for another year and a half. And then we went
back with my mom. We stayed there for three months,
and then we were taken away again. We went back to the

people who lived in the small town, but things didn't go so well in that place, so they moved us to another foster home in that town. Things didn't work out there either, so we got moved to a group home. I stayed at the group home until I left there. After all this time I only figured out one thing: God was still with me. I think about that poem called "Footsteps." Pastor Dan, I'm thirteen years old now, and I found God on my own. He loves me, and I love Him. I prayed for the longest time to be able to go back home. I ended up moving in with my grandparents, but I'm kind of struggling here. It's very hard. I just ask you, PLEASE PRAY FOR ME, WOULD YOU?

That letter just blew me up. I gave it to my assistant and told her, "We've got to find this girl and talk to her." But for three months we couldn't find her anywhere. Then one night at church, this little girl walked up to me again and said, "Hi, I'm that girl who wrote you a letter and handed it to you a few months ago."

I was so glad to see her again, and I turned to listen.

"I have a question for you," she continued. "How can you have hope when everybody in your life has rejected you?"

That little girl had a really good question. It's the same question Joseph must have asked when he was sitting in prison. How does somebody like this little girl live? How do we have hope when nobody wants us?

Well, we have to learn to live beyond our circumstances. That's what Joseph did. He refused to focus on all the rotten things that had been done to him and instead remembered the purpose of God that had been whispered into his heart when he was a teenager. He remembered God. We've got to take our eyes off our circumstances, or we'll never experience the hope of God.

But there's another answer. When we hope in God instead of being overcome by our circumstances, it changes us:

> We have heard of your faith in Christ Jesus and your love for all of God's people, which come from your confident hope of what God has reserved for you in heaven. You have had this expectation ever since you first heard the truth of the Good News. (Col. 1:4–5, NLT)

Did you catch that? What does hope do? It produces faith in Jesus, and it produces a love for other people.

We've got to take our eyes off our circumstances, or we'll never experience the hope of God.

Notice the little word *which* in this verse. It is important. It could also be translated *because of* or *through*. Now catch this. Remember how we saw earlier that faith, hope and love are so important? This little word *which* in Colossians 1:5 shows us how faith, hope and love are tied together. See, the believers in Colossae had *faith* in Christ and a *love* for people, *which* came from their confident *hope* in all that God had stored up for them in heaven. Hope is that important! Hope comes first, and out of hope come faith and love.

These Colossian Christians knew that they had a future, a destiny, that was secure in heaven for them. The hope that this knowledge gave them overflowed in faith toward God and love for others. It is as if Paul was saying to the believers, "I thank God that your unconditional caring, your unshakable commitment, your believing in God, your giving to others, your serving, have all happened to you because of your grasp of hope. You grabbed hold of hope and then said, 'You can do whatever You want with me, God—I'm going to hope in You.'" How do we get love for God and for people? We have confident hope in what God has given us. Do you see that?

When we have confident hope, we can give love to others. But without confident hope in our lives, we have nothing to offer anybody. Our lives are like a mirage. We may offer help to others, but when people who need living water come to get a drink out of our world, they get sand.

Confident hope resides not in our circumstances—it resides in heaven. Our hope is a sealed-up deal, preserved in heaven, because Jesus Christ rose from the dead and totally conquered death. This confident hope in God convinces us that neither life nor death nor angels nor principalities nor powers nor situations in our world nor disappointments in our life nor broken-down washing machines nor lost jobs nor repossessed houses or cars can keep us from the love of God. Confident hope is found in Christ Jesus. When we have that, we are convinced of a hope, an expectation, that's in heaven.

That is what that little girl needs to know. But she's only going to learn it from people who have already figured it out and who have a love for God and a love for other people. That's what the people in the church in Colossae had. And that's what Joseph had—that's why he rose to the top again and again and was able to lead the other servants and prisoners around him.

When we have a hope that resides not in our circumstances but in heaven, my friend, we can help this little girl. When we have this kind of hope, we can help our neighbor. But only when we have a confident hope in God. Not hope in our job, our pay scale or in how many people friend us on Facebook but in the knowledge that God has reserved for us a place in heaven. This verse could be paraphrased, "You have come to grasp these things and they are happening in you because you've gained perspective on something that God Himself gave you of His hope."

Tribulation actually produces perseverance,
and perseverance proven character,
and proven character hope.

The promise is laid up for us in heaven. It's our destiny. Tribulation can never separate us from the love of Christ (see Rom. 8:38–39) or from the fulfillment of God's promise to us. Tribulation actually produces perseverance, and perseverance proven character, and proven character hope. What kind of hope? Hope that does not disappoint.

Christmas ushered in a King. A King of hope. Jesus came to give us life, the fullest life, and to give us a future.

Maybe God has given you a word, a promise, a whisper of His plan for your life. But your circumstances have gone crazy, and nothing has worked out the way you thought it would. But God is saying to you, "Trust Me. Hold on in the pain. Keep obeying Me, keep believing Me."

"But God," you say, "everything around me has caved in. No one wants me. I've lost everything."

God knows our anguish. He knows the long days and weeks and years of pain, and He knows the discouragement and uncertainty we go through. But we can count on His promise to help us:

> At just the right time, I will respond to you. On the day of salvation I will help you. . . . I will say to the prisoners, "Come out in freedom," and to those in darkness, "Come into the light." They will be my sheep, grazing in green pastures and on hills that were previously bare. They will neither hunger nor thirst. The searing sun will not reach them anymore. For the LORD in his mercy will lead them; he will lead them beside cool waters. (Isa. 49:8–10, NLT)

We need to trust. Our obedience and faith will be rewarded, because God's hope does not disappoint. It does not disappoint! When we get through the pain, we will rejoice, because at just the right time we will see a fulfillment of God's promise in our lives.

Will things be hard? Absolutely. Will some of us question God? Of course. But that's the way this works. We hang on even when everything is crashing around us, and then, when we do that long enough, when everybody around us is dying, we'll be thriving. And we will be able to let people know, "Hey, it's going to be okay. We're going to get there. And when we do, it's going to be good."

As we hold steady in our pain, we'll start to figure out that this is God's journey for us. His ways are not ours! The paths that He takes us on will surprise us and maybe even frustrate us at times. But our perseverance will build proven character, and our proven character will manifest in hope that does not disappoint. And our love for God will overflow into other people's lives.

Joseph isn't the only one who understood the need for hope. Look at what David said in Psalm 43:5: "Why are you in despair, O my soul? And why are you disturbed within me? Hope in God, for I shall again praise Him, the help of my countenance and my God." Hope again in God.

The prophet Jeremiah grasped this too:

Remember my affliction and my wandering, the wormwood and bitterness. Surely my soul remembers and is bowed down within me. This I recall to my mind, therefore I have hope. The LORD's lovingkindnesses indeed never cease, for His compassions never fail. They are new every morning; great is Your faithfulness. "The LORD is my portion," says my soul, "therefore I have hope in Him." The LORD is good to those who wait for Him, to the person who seeks Him. (Lam. 3:19–25)

As we walk through the Christmas story, we'll see the message of hope played out in circumstance after circumstance. We'll see how Joseph and Mary banked everything on hope, even when the promise of the coming King's birth completely messed up their worlds. We'll see how the shepherds found hope in the message that that the angel gave them and the joy that they experienced

31

when they followed the angel's instructions to go and see the baby King. We'll see how the wise men's hope led them on a journey of hundreds of miles to worship the King whose birth they had learned about by a star that they had seen in the East.

Christmas is about hope. The newborn King, Christ Jesus our Savior, was a living word of promise and possibility spoken into a dry and dark world. And we can enter into His kingdom of hope if we will get up and trust.

If we want confident hope in God, if we want
His hope to flow out from us to others,
we need to hope beyond our circumstances.

Some of us live in fear rather than in hope, in pain and discouragement rather than in possibility. But there is nobody whose story God does not know. Nobody whose pain God does not know. No situation overmatches God—He can overcome any circumstance. When we are overwhelmed by fear, shame or sorrow, we don't need to stay at the bottom. Even in our deepest despair and hopelessness, there is an answer for us. If we want confident hope in God, if we want His hope to flow out from us to others, we can hope beyond our circumstances, just as Joseph did. We can believe beyond what we feel. We need to get up in the darkness of our night and knock on the door of faith until it opens. We've got to get honest before God and tell Him, "God, I feel hopeless. Could You please impart hope to me again, Lord? Would you let Your grace, Your mercy, be new to me every morning, God? Every,

every morning." As we do this, we will see God's hope manifest in our life.

God wants to release a confident hope in us, a hope that resides not in our pain or in our circumstances but in heaven through the power of His resurrection. Because Jesus was born, because He died, because He rose from the dead, we can live. Nothing can separate us from the love of God that's found in Christ Jesus. We can break free from the power of darkness. We can break free from the power of unbelief. We can stand in the gap for others and believe God to do a deep and healing work in other people's lives so that they can hope again in God. God's mercies and His hope are new every morning.

God sent a King to rule over our circumstances and to give us life. Christmas is for us. Christmas is our story.

JOSEPH AND MARY

Okay, we're going to talk about Joseph and Mary, so get your little pen out, and let's see how you do. Here's your Christmas quiz for chapter 2.

1. Joseph's family had originally come from

   a. Jerusalem
   b. Bethlehem
   c. Nazareth
   d. Chicago

2. When Mary became pregnant, Mary and Joseph were

   a. Married
   b. Facebook friends
   c. Engaged
   d. None of the above

3. When Mary became pregnant,

   a. Joseph left her
   b. Joseph wanted to dissolve the relationship

   c. Mary left Nazareth for a while

   d. The angel told her and Joseph to go to Bethlehem

   e. Both b and c

4. Who directed Mary and Joseph to go to Bethlehem?

   a. Herod

   b. An angel

   c. Caesar

   d. The IRS

5. For the journey into Bethlehem,

   a. Mary and Joseph walked

   b. Joseph walked, Mary rode a donkey

   c. Mary and Joseph rode a bus

   d. Who knows?

6. What did the innkeeper say to Mary and Joseph?

   a. "I have a stable out back."

   b. "Come back after the holidays."

   c. "There's no room in the inn."

   d. Both a and c

   e. None of the above

Here we go, number 1. Joseph's family had originally come from where? Bethlehem. Remember, they had to go back to their home-towns and register. Read your Bibles, okay?

Number 2. When Mary became pregnant, Mary and Joseph were what? Engaged.

Number 3. When Mary became pregnant, what happened? Joseph wanted to dissolve their relationship, and Mary left town. So the answer is e, "both b and c."

Alright, number 4. Who directed Mary and Joseph to go to Bethlehem? Caesar.

Number 5. For the journey into Bethlehem, Mary and Joseph did what? Took the bus? No, they didn't. We don't know how they got there. The answer is d, "we don't know."

And number 6. What did the innkeeper say to Mary and Joseph? Nothing, because an innkeeper is never mentioned in the Christmas story! Trick questions, I know.

We're going to talk about Mary and Joseph's relationship in this chapter. By the time we're done, we'll have these details down.

PRESSING THROUGH TO HOPE

For nothing will be impossible with God.

LUKE 1:37

You've seen them. Nativity scenes everywhere. Joseph and Mary standing or sitting next to a manger. The proud parents lovingly gazing down upon their newborn son, the baby Jesus. Sometimes Mary holds the child. She almost glows with hope. It's all so sweet, peaceful, perfect. Or is it?

In reality, Christmas rocked Joseph and Mary's world. And it should rock ours too. Consider this:

> This is how Jesus the Messiah was born. His mother, Mary, was engaged to be married to Joseph. But before the marriage took place, while she was still a virgin, she became pregnant through the power of the Holy Spirit. Joseph, her fiancé, was a good man and did not want to disgrace her publicly, so he decided to break the engagement quietly. (Matt. 1:18–19, NLT)

I know you've probably heard this story hundreds of times. You may have read it every year at Christmastime just as my family does. You've got it down. Mary was a virgin. She was engaged to Joseph. The Holy Spirit miraculously impregnated her. It was all good!

Keep going. Read the end of the passage again. *Joseph was about to dump Mary!*

"Pastor Dan, this story is supposed to be all nice and Christmassy. Can't we just keep it neat and tidy?" Let me help you with this. There was tension here. Do you feel it? Joseph and Mary were two people in trouble. It was a mess.

> "Pastor Dan, this story is supposed to be
> all nice and Christmassy.
> Can't we just keep it neat and tidy?"

When God works with humans, things usually get messy. We don't have to look any further than Adam and Eve and their encounter with a snake in the garden to figure out why. We are human! And Joseph and Mary were human too.

Let's check out their story. We don't know all the details with any certainty, but this is my take on how things might have gone down.

Joseph and Mary lived in Nazareth. Nazareth is in the northern part of Israel, ninety-one miles north of Jerusalem, near the Sea of Galilee and Mount Tabor. Was it a great place to live? No. It's not even a nice town. Not then and not today. Believe me, I've been there.

What kinds of people lived in Nazareth in New Testament days? Blue-collar workers. Housekeepers, chariot drivers and repairmen. They washed the BMWs, unclogged the kitchen sinks and mowed the lawns of the rich folks who lived in the city down the road. The people of Nazareth never made anyone's most-likely-to-succeed list. They were simple, ordinary. Nothing special. Maybe even suspect.

This city was so unconvincing that the apostle Nathaniel once asked, "Can any good thing come out of Nazareth?" (John 1:46). The answer is barely. Joseph and Mary lived there. They were good. And Jesus grew up there. He was very good—but He had left town. So maybe it was an okay place to be *from*. But not much more.

Joseph and Mary were engaged to be married. "Pastor Dan, Mary was twenty-five or twenty-six years old, a college graduate and the social chair of a local synagogue women's group, right?" Let me paint a clearer picture. Mary was probably between thirteen and seventeen years old. Yes. That's young. But she wasn't like a thirteen-year-old girl of today. Most likely Mary was already working alongside the adults in her home. And she had already reached marrying age. It's true. People back then started everything young, because their life expectancy was only around forty years. Only a few folks made it to fifty. The days when people lived for hundreds of years were long gone.

Joseph was young too. He probably started working when he was around ten years old. He was between sixteen and twenty when he became engaged to Mary.

How do you think Mary and Joseph met? "Well, Pastor Dan, they connected online through eHarmony and fell in love, right?" Not exactly. "Okay, they worked together as baristas at Starbucks, and it was love at first sight." No! Most likely their families knew each other and arranged the marriage for them. The decision was made for the kids. "Well, okay, Pastor Dan, I guess that's how everyone did it back then. So it's all good, no worries. They lived happily ever after!" Not exactly. With human beings life is always tough! People don't just live happily ever after. It's always a struggle. A mess.

"Pastor Dan, you're ruining Christmas." No, I'm trying to make it real. Joseph and Mary lived ordinary lives in a nondescript town. They were real people who worked hard, married young and struggled with real problems. Just like some of us do today. We've got to grasp this. It's real.

Now Mary, despite her humanness, was an amazing young woman. She loved God and was committed to Him. Still, she must have been pretty surprised when one day the angel Gabriel showed up to talk with her: "Coming in, he said to her, 'Greetings, favored one! The Lord is with you'" (Luke 1:28).

The Bible says that Mary was perplexed by the angel's words. "Pastor Dan, I would freak out if an angel appeared and spoke to me!" Yeah, I know. I would have a heart attack and be dead on the floor. Not Mary. She was composed. She was perplexed by the greeting, but she had her wits about her and responded to her visitor as if talking with an angel was an everyday event.

The New King James version tells us that the angel then called her "blessed among women." In the Greek, the angel was saying "God's grace is on your life." Then he told her not to be afraid.

Take note of this: these words that were spoken over Mary are spoken over every single person who knows Jesus Christ. The same words of favor and blessing are used for you and I in the New Testament. These words that the angel spoke over Mary the Spirit of God has spoken over His church. Are you open to receive what the Spirit is saying the way Mary was?

After greeting her the angel told Mary, "You're going to become pregnant! You're going to conceive in your womb, bear a son, and call His name Jesus. He'll be called the Son of the Most High" (see 1:31–32).

After greeting her the angel told Mary,
"You're going to become pregnant!"

I think I'd have been shocked by this announcement. But rather than saying no or exclaiming, "That's impossible!" Mary asked the angel a very logical question: "How can this be, since I am a virgin?" (1:34). The angel answered, "The Holy Spirit will come upon you, and the power of the Most High will overshadow you; and for this reason your holy offspring will be called 'the Son of God'" (1:35, WEY).

It is important for us to understand that the angel Gabriel had been sent by God to a virgin—specifically to this virgin named Mary. God made a huge deal out of Jesus' mother being a virgin. It's not because He is against sex. God made sex, and He is for sex. He gave sexual intimacy to marriage because He thought it was a good idea. But Jesus' mother had to be a virgin, because hundreds of years earlier—seven hundred years, to be exact—God had prophesied that this would be the case: "Therefore the Lord Himself will give you a sign: Behold, a virgin will be with child and bear a son, and she will call His name Immanuel" (Isa. 7:14).

Jesus being born of a virgin would certainly end any speculation about the supernatural purpose of His life. It fulfilled the prophetic requirement of Isaiah 7:14 that declared that the newborn King's birth would be supernatural. Jesus' birth was not a man thing, it was a God thing—only God could have made it happen. And He did make it happen when He miraculously conceived His Son in a virgin.

This was part of God's plan to make Jesus both fully God and fully man. Jesus would be born of a woman, conceived from above. He would be the second Adam who would blot out the disaster brought on by the first Adam: "For God so loved the world, that He gave His only begotten Son, that whoever believes in Him shall not perish, but have eternal life" (John 3:16). Mary certainly had little to no understanding of the enormous meaning behind all that the angel was telling her, but she simply and courageously received everything he said.

Please remember that this was not the first time Mary had to choose to believe something she could not understand. Living in faith and choosing life when the Spirit of God spoke to her had shaped her life up to this point. Mary had walked in faith and obedience for many years before this to become positioned to receive her destiny. Like us, she could have veered to the left or the right at any time and missed out on this great possibility she was being offered of delivering our deliverer. This was certainly a key moment for Mary, but it was only one moment of many in her journey with the Father.

Before the angel left, he told Mary one more thing: "Your relative Elizabeth has also conceived a son in her old age; and she who was called barren is now in her sixth month" (Luke 1:36).

Elizabeth? Six months pregnant? Elizabeth was probably Mary's cousin, maybe her second cousin. She had been barren all her life and was now elderly, so conceiving a child would have been a miracle for her. Now the angel didn't have to tell Mary about Elizabeth. He added that extra tidbit to emphasize what a big deal this entire scenario was to God. To give Mary further confirmation that God's message was true and not some dream. The angel assured Mary, "Nothing will be impossible with God" (1:37).

Mary didn't skip a beat. She accepted the angel's reassurances and replied, "Behold, the bondslave of the Lord; may it be done to me according to your word" (1:38). With that, the angel departed.

Whoa. Do you know what Mary did right there? *She said yes!* What did she say yes to? She didn't really know. She couldn't know. The angel only told her that she would be pregnant and what she was to name her son. No more details. But she must have figured out that when she said yes to pregnancy, she was also probably saying yes to losing her wedding day and her marriage to Joseph. Do you see that? She was engaged, right? But now she was going to have a child before walking down the aisle. That meant no picking out her wedding dress, no sending out invitations, no rehearsal dinner, no exchanging of vows, no first dance. She would lose her dream day, her marriage moment, her reputation and her fiancé. Do you understand? This was big!

"Pastor Dan, that part of the story is not on any Christmas card I've ever seen." No. It's not. But this was reality for Mary. Whenever God moves supernaturally, humans still have to live in the natural. Mary had to. And so do we. Saying yes to God isn't simply a supernatural experience. It always has practical ramifications. It will affect us right where we live.

Remember, Mary was prepared before the angel ever showed up to obey God with her life, no matter what that might have meant. If we figure out how to be prepared for God's word to us— how to say yes to God, no matter the immediate consequences—it will change our destiny. How often do we fight with God when we don't understand something He says to us? Did Mary have a handle on what God was doing? I don't think so. Nonetheless, she responded to God's word with obedience and faith. Do you get everything that God has said to you? I know, the answer is no. How are you responding to Him? With fear or with faith? With frustration or with hope?

If we figure out how to be prepared for God's word to us— how to say yes to God—it will change our destiny.

After the angel departed, Mary arose and decided to rush off to Elizabeth's home in the region of Judea, which was in the hill country. Being a good daughter, Mary may have let her parents in on what was up, but she probably didn't tell them much. Maybe she said, "Mom, Dad, I've got to leave right now. I know you're not going to understand, but I've got to go see Auntie Elizabeth. I'll send you a text message to let you know when I get there safely."

It's a one hundred-mile journey southward from Nazareth to Judea, and Mary probably walked. For the sake of safety, people traveled this route in groups all the time, so it makes sense that Mary may have jumped into one of these caravans.

What thoughts must have been racing through her mind as she traveled! She had to figure out what God was up to. She had to talk with someone who would understand. If she found out that Elizabeth was truly six months pregnant, then guess what? That would be extra confirmation to Mary that she was indeed pregnant too. With a reality this big, Mary most likely could not tell anyone about this except Elizabeth. No one else would have understood. Probably not even Joseph, at least not at this point. All Mary's family and Joseph knew was that she had gone to see Elizabeth. This was the reality.

While she was gone, Mary wasn't Skyping with Joseph or posting Facebook pictures of her pregnant aunt. It's possible, of course, that she sent some kind of message to her parents or to Joseph while she was away, but it's more likely that there was only silence. Mary was a real human being trying to sort out her life, just as you and I do. She was asking God hard questions. She had no idea, really, what God was doing. That's why she left poor Joe in the dark and went up to see her cousin Elizabeth.

Doesn't it make sense that Mary would have wanted to confirm that the angel's message was really was from God before she shared it with others? With something that big, wouldn't you want some verification? That's why she hadn't told anyone why she was going to see Elizabeth. Elizabeth was the only person who could have told Mary, "Yeah, this is really God. You were not hallucinating. This is not a dream. This is real."

Mary arrived in Judah and walked into Elizabeth's house. She had one just question on her lips: "Are you preg—?" But she never got to finish her sentence. The moment she saw Elizabeth, something supernatural happened. Watch this. It says in Luke 1:40–41 that Mary "entered the house . . . and greeted Elizabeth. When Elizabeth heard Mary's greeting, the baby leaped in her womb; and Elizabeth was filled with the Holy Spirit."

Have you ever had a moment when God simply showed up with a demonstration of power? This was one of those moments for Mary and Elizabeth. No words were needed. God just blew up the place. Elizabeth's baby leaped for joy. I wonder what her husband Zacharias thought. Hmm.

Elizabeth obviously had the same spiritual depth and commitment to God that Mary had, although her husband Zacharias had recently had a little faith problem, which we'll see in a bit. Elizabeth, like Mary, was sold out to God. Without skipping a beat, Elizabeth began to prophesy. With a loud voice, she spoke supernaturally over Mary:

> Blessed are you among women, and blessed is the fruit of your womb! And how has it happened to me, that the mother of my Lord would come to me? For behold, when the sound of your greeting reached my ears, the baby leaped in my womb for joy. And blessed is she who believed that there would be a fulfillment of what had been spoken to her by the Lord. (Luke 1:42–45)

Who believed? Who was blessed? That would have been Mary. Now pay close attention. We need to grasp this. We tend to want to be blessed before we believe. But if we're going to walk with God, then when God talks to us, we need first to believe Him, and *then* God will bless us. We need to respond to God with faith. God speaks, we believe, God blesses. That's always how He works.

That's what we see with Mary. Mary wasn't even able to ask, "Hey, Auntie Elizabeth, are you six months pregnant?" because before she could say three words, Elizabeth started speaking over Mary's life. She told her, "Hey, girl, you're going to have a baby, and it's the Son of God." Is that what happened or not? That's exactly what happened. Mary had heard, she had believed, and now she was blessed.

> We need to respond to God with faith.
> God speaks, we believe, God blesses.

Mary's blessing didn't end with Elizabeth's prophetic word. When the Holy Spirit shows up, many people get to prophesy, so Mary jumped right in too. Look at Luke 1:46:

> My soul exalts the Lord, and my spirit has rejoiced in God my Savior. For He has had regard for the humble state of His bondslave; for behold, from this time on all generations will count me blessed. For the Mighty One has done great things for me; and holy is His name.

Who would be counted blessed by all generations? Mary. She was literally speaking about herself. Do you see this? Look what happened next. This girl knew Scripture. She quoted Old Testament prophecy:

> His mercy is upon generation after generation toward those who fear Him. He has done mighty deeds with His arm;

He has scattered those who were proud in the thoughts of their heart. He has brought down rulers from their thrones, and has exalted those who were humble.

Mary spent three months in Elizabeth and Zacharias's home. Why three months? Elizabeth was six months into her pregnancy when Mary arrived—you do the math! That's right, Mary stayed until Elizabeth had her baby.

> Mary showed more faith in her circumstances than Zacharias did in his.

Zacharias, by the way, must have been downright giddy when his son, John the Baptist, was born. He was happy, of course, because he loved his child, but he was also glad to be able to speak again! You see, Mary had shown more faith in her circumstances than Zacharias had in his. When an angel had come to Zach to tell him that he and his aged wife would be having a baby, Zach had been skeptical. Rather than hear, believe and be blessed, as Mary had, Zacharias had heard, feared and been struck speechless until his son would be born. I'm sure he rejoiced at the fulfillment of God's promise in his life!

"Pastor Dan, this is better than a Christmas card. This is a great story!" Let me help you with something. This is a great story unless you're Joseph. Let's catch up with poor Joe. While Elizabeth and Mary were prophesying and the Holy Spirit was moving with power, this guy was sitting back in Nazareth thinking, *what happened to my world? What happened to my girl? She checked out on me. I have no clue what's going on here.* All Joe knew was that Mary had suddenly taken off and didn't appear to be coming back anytime soon. Her unexpected trip out of town must have shaken him up.

"Well Mary went home, Pastor Dan. And she and Joseph kissed and made up." Yes. Mary returned to Nazareth. But let me tell you something. Things were still a mess.

After three months, Mary came home to her family and to Joe. What did she do when she got back? Think about it. She had a serious problem. By this time the girl was three months pregnant. She was starting to show and had yet to break the news about her pregnancy to Joseph. How was she going to do that? "Oh, by the way, Joseph, I need to talk to you about this angel who came to see me. An angel came to me, told me I'm going to get pregnant. I just need to let you know, um, that I'm going to have a baby."

We don't know when Mary broke the news to Joseph. Maybe she hid her pregnancy for a couple more months after she got back. Women wore loose, modest clothing in those days. It would have been difficult to tell when a woman was expecting a baby. Or maybe Mary kept her secret for awhile by wearing some kind of girdle—I don't know. But four or five months into the pregnancy, Mary had to be showing, and she eventually had to break the news to her fiancé.

I can almost hear the conversation. Joseph responds, "Hold it. You're telling me that you're pregnant—and you've been gone for three months. What were you doing up there, girl? This is weird."

Is there a man alive who wouldn't have presumed that she'd been messing around? If your fiancée had been gone for three months and come back and told you that she was pregnant, what would you think? Especially if she told you that she was pregnant by God. Do you think Joseph was blown up or what? He was blown up, big time.

Joseph was devastated. He wanted out of the relationship. He was ready to call off the wedding and put his fiancée away quietly. After all, what else was he supposed to do? Go tell his parents that their future daughter-in-law was pregnant by God? "Oh, Pastor Dan, this is not a good story. This is Christmas, so can't there be a happy ending?" No, my friend. This was real.

If you told your parents that you were pregnant by God, would you expect them to believe you? That's the beautiful dilemma Joe and Mary faced.

Have you ever been squeezed by God?
I don't mean a cuddly, huggy kind of squeeze;
I mean a vice-grip grasp.

God was squeezing Joseph here. Have you ever been squeezed by God? I don't mean a cuddly, huggy kind of squeeze; I mean a vice-grip grasp. When we know God, then at one time or another He will squeeze us. Sometimes He'll squeeze us so hard that we'll wonder, *what are You doing, God? What have I done to deserve this?*

Joseph had to be asking God why. This was not looking like a happy Merry Christmas for Joe. I know, there was no actual Christmas then, but there was no happy or merry anything for this young man. Things were a mess.

God always creates circumstances and situations that we have to respond to with faith. That's how it works. Joe's circumstances seemed impossible—but God was putting his faith to the test.

This is the kind of journey God puts many of us on. Is it a battle? Of course it is. Sudden turns and twists? Absolutely! But unless we wrestle with God's plan for us, we will never really get to see God's promises fulfilled. Likewise, we will never really get to know God.

God always has a reason, a purpose, for putting the squeeze on. We often don't know why He's done things until after He drives us to our knees and we cry out to Him and allow faith to rise up from deep within. And even then, we still sometimes never know the why. But we must trust God. What He does is always for His good and for our good.

Life was messy, but Joseph and Mary had to press through. They couldn't jump ship or bail out. They had to respond to God's word to them in faith. This is our story too. This is exactly how God works today. He tells us things that we flat-out cannot figure out. Then He asks us not to bail out but to give in to Him.

In the midst of the mess, Joseph did some good things. For one, he didn't react too quickly. He held steady. Despite what was probably going through his head, he remained calm.

Hell wants us to be in a hurry. Why? If the enemy can drive us to make decisions too quickly, he can destroy our destiny. Heaven always asks us to wait. How long did Joseph wait? At least three months, maybe longer. His world was upside down. There were no easy answers.

Do you think Joseph was happy during this time? Let's think about it. He was engaged, so that was good. He was excited to be getting married to a beautiful young woman, so that was all wonderful. Then she disappeared for three months, came back and told the guy what? "I'm pregnant." Do you think Joseph was happy now? I think he was angry. I wouldn't be surprised if he yelled at God, "What did I do to deserve this chick? What's up in my world, God?"

Merry Christmas, Joe. This is it. This is your real Christmas story, right here.

Yes, but please get this. Joseph was a witness to God at work. Parting the Red Sea, making a bush burn without burning up, raising people from the dead—lump all these miracles together, and the one Joseph was seeing was greater. Think about it: God inside a human being! This was the single greatest miracle in history, and the guy wanted out. Yes or no? He wanted out. Yes. But did he quit? No. Joe pressed through, despite any fear or doubt or anger he felt.

With some of us, when we get under pressure, our anxiety level gets so high that we freak out and then check out. We turn and run. We scream, "I'm trying to do the right thing, but my world is so chaotic. It's spinning out of control. I've got to take control!" Sometimes we have a pity party and start mumbling to ourselves, "What did I do to deserve this? God doesn't love me anymore, nobody likes me, and Pastor Dan is telling me to do hard stuff!" Yes, it is hard, but guess what happens when we start thinking like this? We abort our destiny.

There are times when we cannot know what God is doing. It's that simple. Then, when we can't figure things out, we want to give up and get out. But we fail to realize that this is just the way God works. He does not tell us what He is doing until we make it through what He's given us to do. We will never know God's intentions until we go through the whole journey and look back.

God is asking us to respond to His word to us with faith. Was there a need for faith in Joseph's life? Yes! We're talking about a need the size of the Grand Canyon here. Don't we need faith as well when we hear something from God that doesn't seem to make sense? What is God asking us to do in those times?

I'll tell you one thing that Joseph didn't do. He didn't say, "Oh yes, God, Merry Christmas. I'm so happy, God, to be in this. I'll just do whatever You want." He absolutely didn't do that. But at the same time, he didn't quit. He struggled for months, but he stayed in. He pressed on through painful days and sleepless nights.

What do you think Joe's friends said when Mary started getting big and showing? "Come on, Joe, what's up, dude? Why are sticking around?" This guy had nothing to win and everything to lose. What could he say to his friends? "Listen, guys, she was up in the mountains with some guy, but she comes back and tells me it's God." What could he possibly tell them to save face?

The Bible says that Joseph was a righteous guy. He probably didn't throw Mary under the bus. But his reputation took a hit. Do you understand that? He got killed. What do you think his father said to him? "Okay, Joe, what have you been doing, son? Fooling around with Mary? I know the temptation—I was a young man once upon a time."

What could Joseph have said to that? "Dad, I didn't do anything wrong. You're blaming me for this whole situation." Joe was in an awkward place. He couldn't win for losing.

Have you ever been totally misunderstood? Have you ever felt that no matter what you say, nobody gets it? How did that go for you? Were you singing "Oh Happy Day" every morning? No. You weren't. It's a miserable place to be. Nobody wants to be in that world. But that was Joseph's world. There was no easy way out for him. That's why he was in such a battle. Of course, at the time he didn't know that he was part of one of the greatest moments in history. That insight could only come with hindsight. That's how God works. That's how He worked with Joseph. And it's how He works with you and me.

Think about the struggles you're dealing with right now. Do you feel that there's no way you can win? Do you want out? It's just possible that God could be doing something supernatural that you cannot figure out. At least you can't figure it out right now. Yes or no?

It's just possible that God could be doing something supernatural that you cannot figure out.

Yes, God just might be up to something. You may be angry, frustrated, afraid. If that is you right now, then go ahead, tell God that you want out. Shout to God in your pain. But stay in. Remain steady. God knows all about us. He knows that we are messy to deal with! That's the truth. God has dealt with human messes for a long time, and He is good at cleaning them up—including yours and mine. Now that's reality.

Do you remember the story that Jesus told about the two sons who were asked to go work in the fields? The first son said, "Yeah, I'll go." And then he didn't go. The second son said, "I'm not going." But then he changed his mind and went without telling his dad. He worked in the field. Jesus asked, "Which son did right?

The one who said he would go and didn't or the one who said he wouldn't go but went?" Which one do you think? What did Jesus say? The second guy. He did right (see Matt. 21:28–32).

When God asks you to do something hard, be the second guy. Go ahead and tell God that you want out. "God, I don't like it. My world has blown up. It hurts!" Say to Him whatever you want to say, but then stay in. Keep steady. Press through, even when you cannot figure God out. Respond to what God is doing in faith and obedience, or you'll abort your destiny. Remember, God is for us (see Rom. 8:31). And if God is for us, then who can stand against us?

So here's how things went for Joseph:

> When he had considered [divorcing Mary], behold, an angel of the Lord appeared to him in a dream saying, "Joseph, son of David, do not be afraid to take Mary as your wife; for the Child who has been conceived in her is of the Holy Spirit. She will bear a Son; and you shall call His name Jesus, for He will save His people from their sins." Now all this took place to fulfill what was spoken by the Lord through the prophet: "Behold, the virgin shall be with child and shall bear a Son, and they shall call His name Immanuel," which translated means, "God with us." And Joseph awoke from his sleep and did as the angel of the Lord commanded him, and took Mary as his wife, but kept her a virgin until she gave birth to a Son; and he called His name Jesus. (Matt. 1:20–25)

Now Joseph had been thinking about breaking up with Mary, but God wanted Joseph and Mary to be husband and wife. God was not going to let Jesus be born illegitimately. Do you see that? In a Hebrew family—and for the prophet's words to be fulfilled—an unlawful birth could not happen. Mary and Joseph needed to be married.

God knew all this, so He had been pushing Joseph for months, trying to convince him to stick with the plan. For months Joseph had said, "No, I want out!" But God finally stepped in and spoke to Joseph in a dream. In the dream an angel appeared to Joseph and let him know that what was happening was all God. That he shouldn't be afraid to take Mary as his wife. What a relief this revelation must have been to Joseph after all his months of struggle! He and Mary still had a tough path to walk, but at least now he knew the truth.

For months Joseph had said, "No, I want out!"
But God finally stepped in.

But when did this dream occur? And when did the nuptials actually take place? This is important to understanding God's dealings with Joseph, so let's try to sort this out.

The Roman emperor had decreed that a census should be taken throughout the empire. Everyone was to travel to their ancestral towns so that they could register for this census. Joseph and Mary lived in Nazareth, but since they were descendants of King David, they had to go to Bethlehem, David's ancient home. It was a one-hundred-mile journey. So Joseph loaded up for the trip, and he and Mary set out.

When Joseph and Mary left for Bethlehem, they were engaged but not yet married (see Luke 2:4–5). So Joseph had his big dream somewhere along the way, and he took Mary immediately as his wife. This means that the couple would have been married when Mary was eight and a half months pregnant.

"Pastor Dan, what about their honeymoon? Did they go on a cruise or visit some cabin at the lake?" Not exactly. The journey to Bethlehem wasn't exactly romantic.

Joseph had wanted out. We know that. And God convinced him to stay. But when did God finally show up, give Joseph a dream and say, "Dude, you're going to marry her"? It was at the eleventh hour, the fifty-ninth minute. God showed up at the last minute. He was late! God always shows up late—or at least it seems that way to us.

And what did God use to convince Joseph to stay in? God used the Word. In Joseph's dream the angel quoted the Old Testament. That must have been some dream! Joseph woke up and said, "Seriously, I'm that guy in the prophecy? We've been taught this story for centuries from the prophet Isaiah, and it's me?" In his spirit he had to have known, "Yeah, the angel is talking about Mary and me. I need to marry her, today."

Of course, God is always with us, and He is well aware of His timetable for our circumstances. But when things are tough and we have to wait a long time to understand God's plan, we grow anxious. We start calling out to Him, "God, hurry up. I'm blown up. My world's falling apart. Where are You?" What does God say to us when we do this? "Just chill out. Listen and wait. If you wait, I'll do My part." And He does His part when? At exactly the right time. Sometimes it's the eleventh hour. But we will make it through the waiting period just fine if we hold onto God's word in faith. It comes back to this: listen, believe, receive.

Remember how steady Mary was when the angel showed up with his surprising announcement? Mary was a virgin, and she was engaged, and the angel Gabriel gave her a word that turned her world upside down. But she received that word. How was she able to do that? Because she had already been living before God in a right way. When God's word came, she was ready to respond to it in a right way. Even though she didn't know what she was getting into, she accepted God's commission. Mary's right living and her right response put her in the right place to receive the miraculous. She received the miraculous touch of God because she was ready to get it. She was positioned for a blessing.

That's why we go to church. We go to hear the Word so that we can make adjustments in our lives and live out of conviction, as Mary did. Then when our moment of truth comes, we too will be able to respond calmly to God in faith and obedience. Did Mary make a decision to be a bondservant of God the day the angel showed up? No! Her decision had been made long before then. She had committed herself to the King long before she received the baby Jesus.

How about you? What decisions are you making? What commitments to God are you settling in your heart? Are you choosing to serve the world or to serve God? These kinds of decisions are strategic in our destiny. They are the decisions that position us for either life and blessing or for despair and discouragement. What we decide on these things will determine what the Spirit of God can give to us and how much we're open to receive from Him. The moment that God shows up to download His seed into our life is not the time for us to decide whether or not we want to receive it. We've got to be ready in advance.

Mary was ready. She was positioned. Most of us are not prepared to receive when He shows up.

Life is sometimes difficult and messy—and totally God. Is it hard? Did God's plan wipe out Mary and Joseph? Yes, it tore them to pieces. It blew their whole world to smithereens. But Mary was ready to receive, and she pressed through. Joseph struggled with what God was doing, but he remained steady in the struggle, and God was there for him at the eleventh hour.

If we're going to walk deep and wide with Jesus, we'd better figure this out. God will ravage us. Sometimes He'll tear us to pieces. We'll look at Him and cry, "But God! Why?"

Jesus explained why. He said, "Pick up your cross, and follow Me" (see Luke 9:23). Let me explain something here. What do you do with a cross? You kill people on it. You crucify people. So what was Jesus telling us? He was saying, "Pick up your cross, and let Me kill you." Why? He tells us that too: "Because unless you die, I cannot live in you" (see Gal. 2:20).

It's worth it to stay in when we want to get out. We're all tempted to quit. But when we stay in, we allow God's story to become our story. Don't give in. Prepare yourself to receive; stay positioned to receive a blessing. Press on. Jesus wasn't a mere baby in a manger. He was the King of the universe. The King of hope—your hope and my hope.

THE SHEPHERDS

When I preached the message about the shepherds in church, a lady sitting in the front row told me, "Pastor Dan, the shepherds were on my Christmas card." I'm happy to tell you something. We are not studying our Christmas cards; we are studying the Bible. We are going to figure this story out. Here we go.

1. How many angels spoke to the shepherds?

    a. A multitude
    b. Two: Gabriel and Michael
    c. One
    d. Who knows?

2. What song did the angels sing?

    a. "O Little Town of Bethlehem"
    b. "Joy to the World" (that would be David Crowder's version)
    c. "Glory to God in the Highest"
    d. "Amazing Grace" (my favorite song—I put this one in)
    e. None of the above

3. What sign were the shepherds to look for?

    a. The star over the stable
    b. A barn outlined with Christmas lights
    c. A baby in a manger
    d. Both a and c

Okay, how did you do this time? Did you get them all? Let's see.

First question. How many angels spoke to the shepherds? A multitude? Two? No, it was only one.

Number 2. What song did the angels sing? The answer is e, "none of the above." The Bible does not say that they sang, just that they praised God. "Trick question, Pastor Dan!" Okay, listen, I think the angels sang when they praised. Do you? If you put c, "Glory to God in the Highest," I'll give you half credit.

Number 3. What sign were the shepherds to look for? A star above the stable? A barn outlined in lights? No, the angel told them that they were to look for a baby in a manger.

Okay, I know that this quiz was a little short, but I made one of the questions a little tricky to challenge you a bit. Did you pass?

Chapter 3

OBEYING THE WORD OF HOPE

*Let us go straight to Bethlehem then, and see this thing that
has happened which the Lord has made known to us.*

LUKE 2:15

Joseph and his very pregnant wife Mary made their way to Bethlehem. Most of us know the story: All the local hotels were packed
out, so Mary had to give birth in a stable, and she laid the baby
Jesus in a manger. Imagine trying to rock your baby in a feeding
trough! Then that night the shepherds came in wonder and awe
and worshiped the newborn King.

But do we really comprehend what happened the night when
Jesus was born? Let's look at what took place in Luke chapter 2:

> [Mary] gave birth to her firstborn son; and she wrapped
> Him in cloths, and laid Him in a manger, because there
> was no room for them in the inn. In the same region there
> were some shepherds staying out in the fields and keeping
> watch over their flock by night. (2:7–8)

While Mary and Joseph were tucked away in their cave, witnessing the miracle birth of the baby Jesus, there were shepherds spending a cold night in the outdoors, taking care of their sheep in the nearby fields.

"Pastor Dan, the shepherds were camping out because it was Christmas Eve, right? Normally they slept at home in their own beds, didn't they?" No, the shepherds slept out in the fields with their sheep every night. All the time. Would you want this job? No, you wouldn't. When it came to employment, the shepherds were at the bottom of the food chain. They could barely make ends meet.

God cares about people who feel as if they're obscure, as if nobody cares about them.

The shepherds were real people with real hassles, just like you and I. We don't see them that way because we see them happily posing in manger scenes around town. "The shepherds are always smiling, Pastor Dan!" Here's a news flash: the real shepherds probably weren't smiling. On the day that Jesus was born, perhaps several sheep had gone astray, a couple shepherds had twisted their ankles running after the wayward sheep, the dinner beans had gone cold, one shepherd's three-year-old child had had a runny nose, and the price of wool had just dropped 60 percent on the stock exchange in Jerusalem. Whew! That was their world!

Can you relate?

These guys were out in the field, obscure, unnoticed, unappreciated—the way some of us feel. Does it seem to you that God doesn't know your name? That He doesn't know your address? That He doesn't care about what's happening in your life?

Here's the truth: God cares about people at the bottom of the food chain. He cares about people who feel as if they're obscure, as if nobody cares about them. Let me assure you. God cares about you. He knows your address. And He is not the NSA!

Some people don't like the Christmas season at all. For some it's a time of pain. All the joy and celebration going on around them just highlights their grief or sorrow or loss. But God is still visiting people's homes.

God hasn't forgotten any of us. It doesn't matter how obscure we feel, how lonely we are, how hidden from everyone else's sight we might be. God knows our pain, our loss, our heartache, our doubts, our depression, our discouragement. God knows our address. And He still makes house calls.

God sends His promises directly into our circumstances. We might feel ignored at Christmas. We might feel lonely or hurt. We might be experiencing grief or sadness or loss. But no matter how forgotten we think we are, we need to be open to receive, because God is still willing to give. God wants to touch us at Christmastime.

Now watch what happened with the shepherds: "An angel of the Lord suddenly stood before them, and the glory of the Lord shone around them; and they were terribly frightened" (2:9).

Why did God choose to show up for these shepherds when He could have announced His Son's birth on CNN or Fox News? Because God cares for ordinary, overlooked people. Don't miss this point in the story. God's choice to visit the shepherds was not accidental. There is purpose here.

God knew the shepherds' address, and on this very first Christmas night, He decided to send a messenger to these guys. The shepherds were probably sitting around a fire, maybe trading war stories from the day, maybe nodding off, when all of a sudden the angel of the Lord was standing right there in front of them, and the glory of the Lord was shining everywhere.

When was the last time an angel showed up to talk with you? "Pastor Dan, we saw it in *Skyfall*. Does that count?" Not quite. That was a James Bond movie, and the angel was a fallen angel!

These shepherds had never seen a movie or a computer-generated image in their life, nor had they speculated about unidentified flying objects. When they saw the bright light, they were probably freaked out. They may have been thinking, *what in the world just happened?* Maybe one or two of them fainted. I would have.

Most of us are afraid of the dark. That night the shepherds were afraid of the light!

Light penetrates darkness. The life of God always flows through the light of God. Jesus said, "I am the Light of the world" (John 8:12). When the light of God shines into our darkness, it freaks us out. We say that we want more of God, but when He shows up in our lives, we are afraid. Do we have reason to be afraid when God shows up? Yes, we probably do, because He wants to change our lives. Even though we want God to change our lives, we're scared to death about what that might mean.

When the light of God shines on us, it does one of two things: it either draws us to God and heals us, or it drives us away. On that Christmas night it totally blew these guys up. They were terribly frightened. "But the angel said to them, 'Do not be afraid; for behold, I bring you good news of great joy which will be for all the people'" (2:10).

That word *great* is *mega* in Greek. Who was this mega joy meant for? All the beautiful people? Is that what the Bible says? We ought to underline that word *all* in our Bibles, because what the angel told the shepherds here broke the mold completely. God was saying to the shepherds, "Jesus didn't come just for the Jews. And He didn't come just for high-society folks. Jesus came for everybody." That's what the angel had just announced. There would be great joy, mega joy, for everybody.

> Today in the city of David there has been born for you a Savior, who is Christ the Lord. This will be a sign for you: you will find a baby wrapped in cloths and lying in a manger. (2:11–12)

A Savior—Christ the Lord, the reigning, ruling King—had been born that day. For everybody. For the shepherds! And the angel obviously expected the shepherds to be excited about it. When the angel spoke to the shepherds, He took for granted that they would go looking for the baby, so He helped them with a sign: "When you go, this will be a sign to you . . ." He told them exactly what to look for.

God gives us signs. The signs are all over the place, but if we are too focused on our own needs or hurts or circumstances, we will miss them.

God has words of promise and hope to speak to us, but our hearts need to be ready and willing beforehand. If they are, then when God speaks, He will assume that we are ready to respond to His lead, and He will give us signs to guide us in obeying Him. God knew that those obscure shepherds, unnoticed by everyone else, would be ready to listen to Him. He knew that they were ready to receive His hope! God knew that the shepherds would even leave their livelihood behind, that they would pay that cost, because God had spoken a word of promise to them. So God gave them a sign.

> And suddenly there appeared with the angel a multitude of the heavenly host praising God and saying, "Glory to God in the highest, and on earth peace among men with whom He is pleased." (2:13–14)

This must have been an angelic choir (even though we don't know for sure that the angels actually sang!). I just have one question: do angels ever sing off-key? Do you ever wonder things like that? Angels are not perfectly created beings. How about you? Do you sing off-key? Would you make it into the angelic choir? Maybe they have a cut list on the angelic choir tryouts. "No, dude, you can't do this. You've got to do another job. You can't carry a tune in a bucket." I hope they have a little grace for people like me who can't sing at all.

The Bible says,

> When the angels had gone away from them into heaven, the shepherds began saying to one another, "Let us go straight to Bethlehem then, and see this thing that has happened which the Lord has made known to us." (2:15)

What did the shepherds say? "That was scary. Let's get outta here!" No. Catch this now—this is significant. What did the shepherds say? When the shepherds suddenly found themselves alone after the angel's surprising appearance, they said exactly what the angel had assumed they would say: "Let's obey right now."

Whenever God speaks, we have to choose to obey.

We need to understand something important here: the shepherds made a choice that night. They could have chosen not to go. In our finite brains we might think, *it's not possible that the shepherds could have rejected the angel's message. They wouldn't have made it on the Christmas cards if they hadn't gone.* But they did have a choice as to whether or not they would obey God, just as you and I do today. Anytime God speaks to us, we have a choice. Any of the shepherds could have chosen to say, "I don't think I want to go. I'm kind of scared of this whole thing. I'm staying in the field."

Some of us do that to God all the time. The Lord speaks to us and says, "Hey, I have this thing for you. I want you to see this. I'd like you to get up and go."

And we say, "I don't think I want to go. That would totally freak me out. I'm going to stay right here."

Whenever God speaks, we have to choose to obey. Because here's what God does: He gives us a word, but He intentionally leaves a gap between the word and the fulfillment of the word. He gives us a promise, He tells us what to do, but we don't see the fulfillment of the promise yet. So there's a gap. What fills the gap?

Our faith and our obedience. God requires us to make a choice: will we believe His word, will we value His promise, and step out in obedience? That's always how it works, friend. Always.

God spoke to the shepherds. He sent an angel to tell them, "Look, there's a newborn baby in a motel in town. You need to go check this baby out." So the shepherds had to decide to get up, leave their sheep on the side of the hill and go into town.

Maybe some of us would have volunteered, "I think I'll stay here. I'll just keep an eye on the sheep. I don't want to go. I'm afraid." Many times the reason that we don't go when the Lord speaks to us is that we live in fear.

But here's the kicker. We need to look at Luke 2:15 again really carefully. What did the shepherds say to each other? "Let us go straight to Bethlehem then, and see this thing that has happened." This little word *thing* is an important one. The word is *rhema* in the original Greek.

In the Greek language there are two words that we translate as the English word *word*. One is *logos*, which typically means "written word." The written word would be the Bible. The other word is *rhema*, which is often translated as "spoken word." This is a personal word that speaks directly into our circumstances. So now we need to rethink what happened with the shepherds. These guys were saying, "Let's go obey this 'living word' that God just spoke to us."

We have God's written word, and we ought to stick our heads in it. We ought to read the Bible every day and let it sink into our minds and hearts. But God speaks personally to us as well. As we walk with God each day, the Holy Spirit will speak living words to us. He'll say, "I would like you to help these people today," or, "I want you to go here today." This is a *rhema* word.

When we hear God speak, we have to decide whether or not we will obey Him. That's what happened to the shepherds. It's what happens in each of our journeys every single day. Jesus said, "My sheep hear My voice, and I know them, and they follow Me" (John 10:27). But some of us don't follow Jesus, because when God talks to us, we say, "If I go into town and knock on the door of the Motel 6 and Jesus isn't there, I won't know what to do!" The shepherds had to get up and go to town. They had to take a risk. It's always a risk for us to obey the word of the Lord, but it's always a risk worth taking.

The shepherds went to a Holiday Inn first. Then they went to the Motel 6, and finally they found the baby over at the Budget Rent-a-Car, right? Actually, if you go into Bethlehem, here's what you'll find. As I mentioned earlier, there are large caves in the area, and in Jesus' day people built inns in front of these caves and then used the caves as stables. Jesus was likely born in one of those caves behind an inn.

But the shepherds had to make a decision. And then they had to put feet to the floor. They had to get up, go to town, knock on doors and say, "Is the kid here? Is the kid here? Did you guys have a baby here lately?"

This is central for our journey and our destiny: the way God worked with the shepherds is the way God always works. He gives us a chance to enter into partnership with Him by calling us to step out in faith and obey the living word that He has spoken to us. God will speak a promise to us and say, "Now get up out of your comfy armchair and go!"

Some of us say no. God speaks to us a *rhema*, a "thing," a living word, and tells us to go here or do this thing or talk to this person.

"But God," we say, "I can't see over there. I don't know how to get over there!"

The problem is, every time we say no, we lose destiny. Every single time. We lose hope, and we lose promise and possibility, because we never connect the dots from God's promise to our faith and obedience to the fulfillment of the promise.

We watch other people connect the dots. We see people get a *rhema* word from God, obey the word in faith and experience a supernatural touch from God. But we hang back in fear.

Just go. Get up and go. When we obey, God will help us find our way, and when we get to where God has told us to go, we will rejoice, because we will experience a fulfillment of God's promise inside us.

> Just go. Get up and go. When we obey,
> God will help us find our way.

"But what about my sheep? I can't just leave them here on the hillside alone! And besides, it's late, and I'm tired, and I'm not sure where the baby is anyway . . ."

Don't complain. Just go! Yes, it will be hard. Yes, the way might be unknown to us. But that's the way this works. We go where God tells us to go, and when that becomes the pattern of our life, we will be able to strengthen others around us who are having a hard time obeying. "It will be okay," we can tell them. "Let's go! We can make it! And when we do, we'll see the amazing thing that God has for us."

So what happened to these guys when they went?

The shepherds "came in a hurry and found their way to Mary and Joseph, and the baby as He lay in the manger" (2:16). Was anybody cured from cancer that night? Was anybody raised from the dead? Did they see any great supernatural miracle? I don't think anything like this happened. Let's read it again: "They came in a hurry and found their way." That means that they knocked on doors. "Oh Pastor, surely they had a GPS to help them find the baby." No. The shepherds didn't have supernatural revelation to help them find the baby King. They had to search through the community and look for Him. And they found the baby lying in a manger.

> When they had seen this, they made known the statement which had been told them about this Child. And all who heard it wondered at the things which were told them by the shepherds. (2:17–18)

Often when God speaks a living word, the "thing" He tells us is meant to be spoken into other people's lives too. The Christmas story is not only for a select group of people; the Christmas story is for all people! God's good news of great joy, His hope and destiny and purpose, are for everyone, and that good news should fill us with such joy and hope that it overflows from us to others.

Christmas itself is a *rhema* word from God to all of us, isn't it? The baby King was for everyone. His coming to earth is a story of hope for us to hear and then to share with others.

Look again at what the shepherds did. The New Living Translation puts it this way: "After seeing him, the shepherds told everyone what had happened and what the angel had said to them about this child." When God speaks to us words of promise, He wants us to share them with the people around us. He wants to use us to touch other people's lives.

Here's the tragedy. Some of us are too busy doing our own thing. "I have my family Christmas traditions, Pastor Dan! We're going to the Nutcracker. We've got a million gifts to buy!" But remember—the story of Christmas is that "God so loved the world, that He gave His only begotten Son, that whoever believes in Him shall not perish, but have eternal life" (John 3:16). *Whoever* means everyone who wants to! God is crazy about each and every one of us. The ordinary people, the humdrum people, the lonely people—everyone. But people can't believe in Jesus if they never hear about Him.

Do you know what God's *rhema* word in the story of Christmas is? By giving us His Son to rule and reign in each of our worlds, God was telling every single person on earth, "I'm crazy about you!"

But when we hear God speak, we often don't respond—we're too busy with our work, too worried about our financial concerns, too focused on our pain or grief or fear. Simply put, we won't surrender our heart and lay down our life.

Christmas is about real people being really touched by a real God. Christmas speaks to us the hope of the gospel, and God wants to speak that word through us into other people's lives.

Now watch Luke 2:19: "Mary treasured all these things, pondering them in her heart." We should underline this verse in our Bibles. Even though it's true that we are supposed to share the story of Christmas and hope with everyone, there are times when God speaks to us a living word, a personal word, and we aren't supposed to tell anybody what God has said to us. Don't put it on Facebook!

What happened to Mary? The Bible says that she hid all that was happening in her heart. Mary's word from God was not like the gospel message, which was intended to be shared with everyone. Hers was a personal word from God about who Jesus was and all that He would one day become. If we want God to tell us secrets, we'd better learn to zip our lips, because sometimes we're not supposed to tell anybody the vision God whispers into our heart.

Remember our friend Joseph in the Old Testament? The same phrase that was used to describe Mary's action is used of Joseph's father Jacob. Joseph, as we know, had two dreams. The first time he had a dream, he put his dream on Facebook and told his brothers all about it. And it got him into all kinds of trouble.

After his second dream, he did it again. He told his brothers what he'd dreamed! And this time he told his father Jacob too. You know what his dad said? "I think you're nuts, kid. Do you really think your whole family is going to bow down to you one day?" But then the Scripture says this: "But his father kept the saying in mind" (Gen. 37:11). In other words, he hid it in his heart. Jacob sensed, "There's something supernatural going on with this kid. I'm not sure what it is, but I need to watch it" (see Gen. 37:5–11).

That's exactly what the Scripture says about Mary. It says that Mary couldn't figure out what was going on with this child who had been born as a King. She didn't understand it all, so she hid it in her heart.

We need to hide some of the things God tells us. Not everything we hear from Him is meant for public consumption. God speaks quiet words to us so that we can pray about them, so that we can watch for the fulfillment of His promise—but we are not supposed to talk about them. We write them in our journal and keep them between ourselves and God.

Now let's see what the fulfillment of the shepherds' promise looked like: "The shepherds went back, glorifying and praising God for all that they had heard and seen, just as had been told them" (2:20).

Whoa! Hold it. The shepherds had been given a living word from God, and they'd gotten up and obeyed—and guess what happened? They had connected the dots between God's word and God's fulfillment—they filled the gap with faith and obedience—and they saw the word of God turn to promise.

Does this happen for people who live in fear? No, it does not. Why? Because fearful people will never fill the gap with faith and move ahead. They will remain paralyzed back in the field with the sheep. "Look," they say, "we were way freaked out by those angels. We just need to stay here and recover."

We need to lay aside our fear and instead declare, "Let's obey what the Lord has spoken. Let's go see what God is doing and then leave rejoicing!"

The Greek word for *rejoicing* is *doxazo*. The word *doxology* comes from it. *Doxazo* means "praise and adoration to God." It comes from the Greek word *dokeo*, which means "to believe." Do you know what happened that day when the shepherds saw the baby Jesus and went away rejoicing? Their faith level went higher! Their hope level went up! They believed God, and they ended up praising God and full of hope! Did circumstances change in their world? Did the price of wool go up? No, I don't think so, but their hope went up.

When the Lord speaks to us and we trust Him, our hope goes up. And when that happens, everything in our life changes, because we gain perspective on our own little world. We see our own story in God's much bigger story. But we've got to obey.

> When the Lord speaks to us
> and we trust Him, our hope goes up.

When God gives us a living word, a *rhema* word, and we don't obey, we get discouraged. We watch other people obey and get blessed, and we go to God and complain, "God, why don't You do something for me? Why don't You help me?" And God says, "Why don't you go? I gave you a word, but you didn't trust Me. Why don't you follow through and get blessed?" When we obey God's word, we come back glorifying and praising God, and our faith level is raised.

The shepherds rejoiced, didn't they? But get this: Fear and rejoicing don't live together. Fear and promise don't live together. Fear and possibility don't live together.

How did the shepherds end up rejoicing? Because hope and joy live together. Hope and rejoicing live together. The shepherds were able to rejoice because they rejected fear and embraced hope, and they saw the promise of God fulfilled.

Human beings live and die on hope. That's why the Bible says that there are three things of greatest importance: faith, hope and love. And these three things are tied together. We saw that in Colossians 1:4–5 earlier in this book: "We heard of your *faith* in Christ Jesus and the *love* which you have for all the saints; because of the *hope* laid up for you in heaven." Without hope, we have no faith. Without hope, we cannot love God. Without hope, we cannot love others. We just can't do any of it. We need fresh hope every day. Thankfully, God's mercies are new every morning.

Does the Bible mention the shepherds again after the Christmas story? Ever? No, never. Why did God announce His Son's birth to these ordinary, forgotten guys? Because they were just like you and me, that's why. They were people who counted. They didn't count to everybody, but they counted to God. And so do we.

God knows our address, friend. God knows where we're living. God knows our pain. God knows our circumstances. And He knew all these things about each one of those shepherds. Nobody else in their society cared about them. Nobody else wanted to hang out in the fields with them. The reason there are shepherds in the Christmas story is because God wanted to tell you and I something through them: "I always watch you. You are not obscure to Me. You may feel anonymous, but you're not. I know your name, I know your address. I know your pain. I know what is happening in your world."

"Yeah, but Pastor Dan, the shepherds had all kinds of opportunities that we never get. They had a star to lead them right to the baby!" Really? Did the star lead them to the manger? "Pastor Dan, it's right there on my Christmas card. The star is right there over the baby and Mary and Joseph and the shepherds." Listen, the star didn't lead the shepherds to the manger. If you have a Christmas card with a star leading the shepherds to the manger, throw it in the trash. It's the wrong story. The star led the wise guys.

God gave the wise men a star because they traveled for many, many months. That's why they needed a GPS. The shepherds only had to travel a few miles. They just had to walk into town.

You know who led the shepherds? The Spirit of God. They had to get up and follow the Holy Spirit's lead!

I don't know how far you and I will have to walk to connect the dots by faith between God's *rhema* word to us and its fulfillment. But we'll have to go somewhere, and we'll have to depend on God's leading. That's just how this works. We've got to get up and go. God will give us a word in oder to give us a possibility. And when we move, He'll raise our hope level and our faith level. If we don't move, we won't get hope.

If we're going to understand what hope is, we've got to understand what it's not. Hope is not wishful thinking. Hope is not daydreaming. Hope is not positive thinking or optimism. None of these are necessarily bad things; optimism and positive thinking can change our attitude. But they won't change our world. They won't address our problems. They won't heal our hearts and lead us into God's purpose for our lives.

Optimism is psychological—it changes what's in our head. But hope is theological—it changes what's in our heart. Optimism is positive thinking, but hope is passionate trust. There's a gigantic difference between the two. Now being optimistic in our thinking is a lot better than thinking negatively. But hope goes deeper than optimism. Hope is firmly placed in something substantial. And that something substantial, the Bible tells us, is God. When we hope in God, we gain perspective on our world that we could never find through mere positive thinking.

Optimism says about our circumstances, "Well, it's not so bad." It can actually deny reality. Hope says, "No, things are really bad. But God's really big." God is really big. We believe in a God who's greater than all our bad circumstances.

Every one of us has a story. Some of our pain levels are at nine and ten right now; others of us have pain levels at two or three. But everybody has a story. And no matter what it is, our story doesn't remove us from God's possibilities. God is greater than all our stories. God is greater than all our pain. God is greater than all our circumstances. But we've got to believe. We've got to step out in faith and obey when the Holy Spirit says to us, "Here's what I'm speaking to you. Trust Me. Walk with Me, and watch Me touch you. Watch Me change you. Watch Me show up."

We've got to get our eyes off our circumstances. "But Pastor Dan, life is so hard. Things are so bad!" Maybe that's true. But did God show up for the shepherds? Absolutely. And what did they end up seeing? A baby. They saw a promise. A promise fulfilled.

That's what God will give us. He'll speak to us a *rhema* word for our own circumstances. Then, when we obey His word, He'll fulfill His promise to us. When that happens, we will begin to live in expectation and in hope that something bigger is coming our way.

Fill the gap with faith and obedience, and watch God fulfill His purpose in your life.

THE WISE MEN

How have you done on the quizzes so far? When I gave them at church, everyone flunked. Now, if this encourages you at all, I gave the quizzes to our staff members at our Christmas party, and they flunked too. Maybe you'll do better. Are you ready? In this chapter we'll look at the wise men. So let's see what you really know about these guys.

1. Who saw the star over Bethlehem?

    a. Mary and Joseph
    b. The shepherds
    c. The three wise men
    d. Both b and c
    e. None of the above

2. How many wise guys came to see Jesus?

    a. An army
    b. Three
    c. Twenty-six
    d. None of the above
    e. All of the above

3. What in the world are magi?

    a. Eastern kings

    b. Magicians

    c. Astrologers

    d. Guys wise enough to follow the star

    e. Theologians

4. When the wise men brought their gifts to Jesus, they found Him in

    a. A manger

    b. A house

    c. Vacation Bible School

    d. Motel 6

    e. None of the above

Number 1. Who saw the star over Bethlehem? You don't know? The answer is e, "none of the above." Uh-oh, you are flunking already. "No, Pastor, it was the three wise men!" Don't worry. We're going to study the wise men in this chapter so that we can get this right, okay? There were not three wise men mentioned in the Bible. There were three gifts mentioned in the Bible. And none of the other folks even hinted at seeing the star.

Number 2. How many wise guys came to see Jesus? The Bible doesn't tell us how many. It only says that they brought three gifts, so we don't know. You flunked again! But that is okay. That is why I needed to write this chapter.

Number 3. What in the world are magi? Well, now this one is interesting, because the answer could be either a, "Eastern kings" or c, "astrologists." It's a little debatable. So if you put either a or c, I'll give you credit, because you might need the points, and this book is about finding hope in the midst of despair.

Number 4. When the wise men brought their gifts to Jesus, they found Him where? In a house. Jesus was a toddler by the time the wise men came, not a baby, so his parents had moved from the cave to a house.

How did you do?

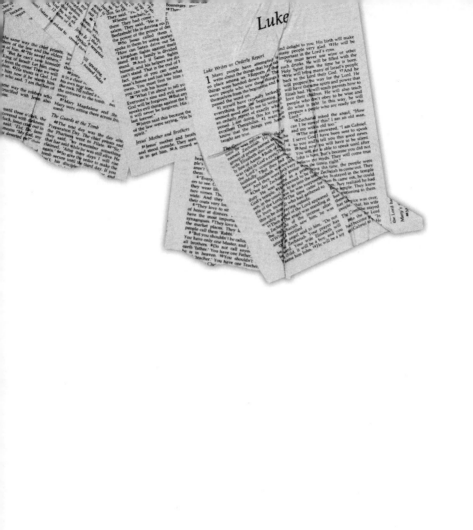

Chapter 4

FINDING HOPE IN HARD TIMES

Where is He who has been born King of the Jews?
For we saw His star in the east and have come to worship Him.

MATTHEW 2:2

I once rode a camel. Don't do it. Believe me, it's not like riding a horse. There's a big hump in the middle of a camel's back, and you must carefully balance yourself—or slide off. My camelback journey lasted only a quarter of a mile, but it was sheer agony. I have a photo to prove it.

The wise men of the Christmas story traveled on camels a thousand miles to Israel—and then another thousand miles back home again. Their journey probably took one year each way. How in the world they did it, I don't know. Of course, if I were going to see the baby Jesus, then I could bear climbing on a camel's back. But you will not find me on a camel again for any other reason.

The wise men, of course, had seen a star in the sky and had followed it across the desert. They went looking for the newborn baby who would fulfill prophecy to become the King of the Jews. "Pastor Dan, I know this story, because we see the wise men standing right next to the shepherds and animals in the manger scene. There are three of them!" Uh-oh. Here we go again. How many times do we have to go over this? The wise men were never at the manger, and we don't know how many of them came to see baby Jesus. Let's check out the story:

> Now after Jesus was born in Bethlehem of Judea in the days of Herod the king, magi from the east arrived in Jerusalem, saying, "Where is He who has been born King of the Jews? For we saw His star in the east and have come to worship Him.". . . After coming into the house they saw the Child with Mary His mother; and they fell to the ground and worshiped Him. Then, opening their treasures, they presented to Him gifts of gold, frankincense, and myrrh. (Matt. 2:1–2, 11)

When we read this passage, we tend to think that the wise men just hopped on camels and went for a ride. That's not exactly what happened. Traveling so far and for so long would have required a lot of preparation and would have been a huge step of faith. It would have been a major test of their commitment to God.

The wise men had to leave their homes, families and everything that was familiar to them. They knew when they left that they would be away for two years and would face serious dangers along the way. But they had seen the star in the sky, and they knew what it meant. A King was born. They had no choice. They had to go.

How did the wise men know about the star and the baby? Let's have a brief history lesson. The wise men, or magi, probably lived in Persia. That's modern-day Iraq. Over the centuries the Hebrews (the Jewish people) and Persians had crossed paths many times. In fact, the Persians once freed the Hebrews from evil Babylonian captivity when they conquered the Babylonian empire. That happened more than five hundred years before the wise men saw the star. Some Hebrews returned to their homeland in Israel after this took place, but some remained in the now-Persian empire. Because of this the wise men had the Hebrew Bible, which is our Old Testament. There's no doubt that many Persians knew about and worshiped the God of Israel.

The magi, being astrologers and wise men, had clearly observed through the Hebrew writings the prophecies regarding the coming Messiah.

The magi, being astrologers and wise men, had clearly observed through the Hebrew writings the prophecies regarding the coming Messiah. Then, when the star appeared, they came to realize that it was a sign of the new King's birth. But making the decision to hit the road was only their first test. There would be another test to come. A big one. Just wait and see what was going to happen with these guys!

The magi caravan that traveled from Persia to Israel must have been rather large—not the charming three-camel unit we see bobbling along on Christmas cards. After all, these guys had to carry ample supplies for the long journey. And then there were the gifts they planned to bring along. They needed a large enough entourage to keep them from being picked off by robbers. Journeying to Israel was a gigantic undertaking for the wise men.

Once on their way, the star led the caravan to Jerusalem. What a thrill it must have been when the magi spotted the city gates. After one very long year on the backs of camels, the star had finally led them to their destination! As soon as they were inside the city of Jerusalem, the wise men started asking questions. They walked in and wanted to know, "Where is He? Where's the baby King?"

The guy in charge, the wicked King Herod, said, "What baby? We don't know what you're talking about."

Uh-oh. "Houston, we have a problem!"

The magi had expected to see the newborn King, but instead they got zilch. How would you have felt if you had bumped along on the back of a camel for a year expecting to see the newborn child only to arrive at your destination and be told there was no baby? Your gut response would likely have been to climb back on your camel, pull the reigns and head home. This was a real test for the wise men. A hard test. Just when they thought that their hope was about to become reality, it seemed to vanish.

Isn't this exactly how God sometimes tests us? He gives us insight. He calls us to a certain place in our destiny. But He doesn't snap His fingers and, poof, we are there. No, that isn't how He works. God expects us to get up off the couch and go. We have to step out and trust Him. And we have to seek Him and listen for His continued leading along the way. It takes faith.

Could God have put the baby Jesus in Jerusalem? Couldn't He have just told the magi that the baby was in Bethlehem? Had God intentionally led these guys to Jerusalem knowing that Jesus wasn't there? The answer to all of the above is yes.

I think that God intentionally led the wise guys to Jerusalem before taking them to Bethlehem. He wanted to see how they would respond. I have seen God do this in my own life. It will happen in yours too. Sometimes God leads us somewhere. We take the big step of faith and start moving. Maybe we move for a long time. Then, when we arrive, the place doesn't look at all like what we'd expected it to. We start asking, "What's up, God? I thought You told me that this or that was going to happen. Where are You? I'm so confused."

When our expectations don't match reality, we're disappointed. Even perplexed. Maybe we're tempted to be mad at God. And we have questions. Lots of questions. Did we hear wrong? Was our GPS setting off? Did God change His mind? Does God still love us? Now what do we do?

God speaks to every one of us. At some time or other in the course of our walk with Him, He puts a word or a sense of His leading in our hearts, and He births destiny in us. He stirs up purpose in our lives. So how do we know that the word we hear is really Him speaking to us? How do we know that we're on the right track in our attempts to follow Him?

God has been speaking for a long time. When He created the world, He spoke. When He created Adam and Eve, He spoke. When He created you and me, He spoke. God creates by speaking. And when He speaks to us, He creates destiny in our lives.

What has God said to you about your world?

God didn't speak just once when He created the world. He's still talking today. The question is, will we hear what God says to us about His plan for our lives? And if we hear it, will we understand it? If we understand it, will we believe it and act on it?

How does God speak?

Now I know that we've jumped back to the story of the other Joseph in the Old Testament a lot in this Christmas book—but Joseph was a wonderful picture of Jesus and of the hope the King came to bring us. If anyone knew God's voice speaking to Him, it was Joseph. God spoke His will and destiny into Joseph's life through a couple of dreams when Joseph was only a teenager. But then what happened to our boy?

=====

Joseph was a wonderful picture of Jesus and of the hope the King came to bring us.

=====

Well, just as He did with the wise men, God tested Joseph. It wasn't long after God spoke into Joseph's heart that things went downhill for him really fast.

Tests always last as long as God wants them to last. Maybe you have been stuck in a situation for a long time. It could be that your own disobedience has gotten you stuck between a rock and a hard place. But if you are walking with God, like Joseph and the wise men were, maybe you have been boxed in by tough circumstances, and you're wondering how in the world you ended up where you are. If this is you, God has purposely put you there to test you.

The question is, will you be patient and wait? Joseph did. And look what happened! He pretty much ended up running Potiphar's house and later the whole prison. What sustained Joseph through thirteen years of unjust suffering at the hands of his own family and of foreigners? He never let go of the assurance that God's promise to him would one day come to pass.

It's worth it for us to take a few moments to look at some of the details of Joseph's story. Psalm 105:17–19 gives us a summary of the testing Joseph endured: "[God] sent a man before them, Joseph, who was sold as a slave. They afflicted his feet with fetters, he himself was laid in irons; until the time that his *word* came to pass, the *word* of the Lord tested him" (emphasis added).

Note those two uses of the word *word*. What makes this verse so insightful for us is that these two uses of *word* have different Hebrew meanings. The first meaning, in the phrase "his word came to pass," is *dabar*. This word is used 1,439 times in the Old Testament and is usually translated "spoken word." The second meaning, in the phrase "word of the Lord tested him," is *imrah*. This word appears only thirty-seven times and means "written word" or "commandment."

So here is what the verse actually says: "Until the time that his *spoken word* [his dreams] came to pass, the *written word* [the commandments] of the Lord tested him." In other words, God had given Joseph a spoken word, a personal word of destiny, with those two dreams. It was a promise spoken into Joseph's heart by God. But the time for its fulfillment was a long way off. In the meantime, God wanted to do some testing in Joseph's life, and that testing would be done through God's written word—His commands. Once Joseph passed the test of keeping God's written word, then God would bring about the fulfillment of His spoken word.

Follow me on this one, because the difference between these two uses for *word* is important, and understanding it will help us hear God better in our own lives.

For Joseph, the spoken word of God to him, his *dabar*, was through two dreams. "But Pastor Dan, how did the written word test him? Joseph didn't have a Bible with him in Egypt!" No, he didn't. But Joseph knew God's *imrah*, God's commands. He had been taught God's written word all his life. He knew the commands and laws of God, what pleased God and what did not.

Now watch this. When Pharaoh's wife came along and tried to get this handsome young kid to go to bed with her, what did he do? Did he freak out? Does it appear that he even considered her request? No. Joseph didn't think about it. He didn't waffle. He just said no. Period. Joseph didn't need a dream to know what he should do in this situation. He knew his Bible, so when the test came, he knew how to act. He knew what was right and what was wrong, so he passed the test.

God puts all of us in situations that test us. He does it on purpose. At home, at school, at work—yes, even at church! He gives us a *dabar*, a spoken word—a promise in our heart. Then, when the test comes, we find out how well we know the *imrah*, the written word—the things in the Bible. We find out whether or not we will apply the principles of God under pressure. And we flunk this test a lot of times! Then we get to be tested again. Kind of like when we're trying for our driver's license or when we take the quizzes in this book!

So the written word (the Bible) tested Joseph, but he didn't get released from his test until the spoken word (his dreams) came to pass. Getting this down is vital.

All of us have the written word. The Bible. The Holy Spirit speaks to us through the Bible. But He also speaks specifically into our life. Do you remember how in the last chapter we learned about the *logos* (the written word) and the *rhema* (the spoken word, the living word)? The shepherds received a *remah* word, a "thing," telling them about the baby Jesus. Do you notice any similarities here? *Logos* and *dabar* both mean "written word," and *remah* and *imrah* both mean "spoken word." The principles are very much the same.

Imrah is like *logos*. Written down. *Dabar* is like *remah*. Spoken in.

What did the wise men have? Well, think about it. They had the *imrah*, the *logos*, in which they read the prophecies about the Savior who would one day be born. Then they had a *dabar*, a *remah*, from God in the appearance of the star. They knew that the star was a personal word from God for them to take up the arduous journey to Israel so they could worship the world-changing baby King.

Some people don't believe that God speaks personally, but that only means that they cannot hear Him.

Some people don't believe that God speaks personally, but that only means that they cannot hear Him. He does speak. He speaks to people who have a living relationship with Him. Our God is alive. In the verse in which Jesus said, "My sheep hear My voice" (John 10:27), the word for *voice* is *remah*. Jesus was talking about a word that gives us personal direction, a word that is for each of us individually and not for anybody else. This is what Joseph received in his dreams and what the wise men received when they saw the star.

Anyone who is truly following Christ will want to be vibrant for Him (Romans 12:11 calls it "fervent in spirit"). But in reality, we will be excited about God only if He's speaking to us and if we are hearing what He has to say. If we want a fervent relationship with Christ, we have to take the time to listen to His voice.

The renowned preacher A. W. Tozer once wrote, "If we do all the talking when we pray, how will we ever hear God's answers?" Tozer makes a great point! Some of us never take time to listen. So we become frustrated. If the wise men hadn't taken time to stop, pray and listen to the voice of God, they would never have embarked on their journey to Israel. And when they found themselves being tested in Jerusalem, unsure about where to go next, if they hadn't waited for the next word from God, they would have been on the path back to Persia without ever traveling those last four miles. They would have decided the next step for God rather than letting Him direct them to the feet of Jesus.

If we want a fervent relationship with Christ, we have to take the time to listen to His voice.

You and I need to believe that God will speak to us. That He has a word for us. And that His word will transform us. "But Pastor Dan, what if He tests me? What if He takes me to some way-out place and things are hard and I get stuck?" Yes, God will test us. Yes, we might feel confused. But if we know the *logos*, the *imrah*, the Bible, and if we hold onto God's *dabar*, His *remah* word in our hearts, and refuse to doubt, we can trust God to keep speaking to us and to guide us to the fulfillment of His promise! And to make us more mature and useful believers along the way.

God builds character in us before He releases us into great possibility. If we don't pass the character test, then we won't get the release. If we want our world to get bigger, we need to have our character developed.

The prophetic, the *dabar*, tests our faith. Will we hold on to God's promise, no matter how long it takes to come about, no matter how confusing the path may be? The written word, the *imrah*, tests our character. Will we obey God's commands in the time of testing while we are waiting for His promise to be fulfilled?

We need to remember God's prophetic *dabar* word to us during hard times. When Joseph was in jail, he could have become bitter. Instead he became better. He thought, *I'm not going to give up, because I had those dreams from God. There's something about those dreams.* When the wise men arrived in Jerusalem after following the star for a year and found out that the baby they were seeking was nowhere to be found, they thought, *we know from God's Word and from the star that God spoke to us. He must have the next step for us.* They didn't give in to their circumstances. They believed what God had spoken.

We need God to speak into our world so that we can trust Him when things get really difficult. He will establish us, He will transform us. How will He do it? By speaking into our life. As much as we will listen, God will talk.

But before we hear a living, personal word from God, we should be grounded in the Bible. If we don't know God's written word, then when we hear prophetic words, we won't know who's talking to us.

First Corinthians 13:9 declares, "We know in part and we prophesy in part." "What does that mean, Pastor Dan?" It means that people can give us words from God, but people are fallible. People don't always get it right. And even when they get it right, people don't know the whole for our lives—only a part. We know in part, and we prophecy in part.

We need to be wise when someone speaks a word to us that he or she believes is from God. We should never take what someone speaks to us and try to live it out. We aren't the ones who will fulfill a prophetic word—God does that. And we can't shape our life around one word anyway. By nature, a personal word is only in part—it's not the whole. If we try to make it the whole or even the centerpiece, we'll get ourselves in trouble. Prophetic words will confirm what the Spirit is already saying to us. We follow the Spirit, not the prophetic word.

We have to test the words we receive. First Corinthians 14:29 warns us to test prophecy. A person should never say, "God told me to tell you this or that." He or she should say, "I think God might be saying this to you." God does give us personal words through other people, but we need lots of room to test that word against the written word and to be sure that we are hearing from God directly.

The written word, the Bible, is in whole; the prophetic word is in part. People's words are fallible, but God wrote the Bible, so it's infallible. The problem is that a lot of us don't read our Bibles, so we end up chasing any voice that comes our way. The Holy Spirit wrote the Bible, so when the Holy Spirit speaks to us, He'll never say anything that contradicts the Bible. If we know our Bible, if we read it and feed off it, we'll know God's voice when He speaks destiny into our lives.

Joseph's life and the wise men's lives were touched by the word of God prophetically. God spoke into their circumstances supernaturally. And then He tested them. It can be very hard when God bends us as He did them, but there is a plan to all the wildness that happens in our lives. When God bends us, our ears get really big. We become ready to listen. When God speaks, yes, there will be pressure. But when God moves, there is no other release like it anywhere in this world.

> When God bends us, our ears get really big.
> We become ready to listen.

The magi probably asked all of sorts of questions once they learned that the baby Jesus was not in Jerusalem. They must have been thinking, *why did we just waste a year of our lives? Now we look foolish.* At that moment, of course, they had no idea that they were just four miles away from their destiny—that baby Jesus was just down the road in Bethlehem.

"Pastor Dan, if they had gone home, they wouldn't be part of the Christmas story today." That's right. We wouldn't know magi from reindeer. They would have missed their destiny like some of us are missing ours right now. This is exactly how God works. He speaks prophetically into our life, asks us to obey, and then sends us on our way. He tests us.

"Well, Pastor Dan, I like the part about getting a personal word. But I don't like this bit about testing. I don't think it's fair!" I'm not sure *fair* is the right word here. There is no "fair" verse in

99

the Bible. Life isn't fair, and neither is God. He is in the business of building life-giving people who often have to suffer along our journey in order to be able to comfort and bring life to others. God is God. He can do whatever He wants with us. Just remember, though, that God is just. And loving. What sometimes appears to be a letdown to us may actually become a blessing. God always fulfills His promises. He just fulfills them in His way, not our way.

That's one reason our expectations don't always match God's results. We are supposed to read our Bibles, listen to God's word to us and then step out in faith. Too often we listen but then try to fill in the blanks ourselves. When the star disappears, we start applying our own logic to the situation. We go off on our own and end up missing God's destiny for our lives.

Walking in this way can be dangerous and difficult. The Bible is full of stories of people who got a word or a promise from God and then rushed off to fulfill that word themselves. From Abraham to Moses to Peter we see good, godly people sometimes attempting to fill in the blanks instead of waiting on the Lord to do things His way. There is a bit of good news here though. Jesus is excellent at unwinding our ideas if we will let Him. God's Word assures us,

> The vision is yet for the appointed time; it hastens toward
> the goal and it will not fail. Though it tarries, wait for it;
> for it will certainly come, it will not delay. (Hab. 2:3)

The tests God gives us are not the kind in which we memorize the answers, fill in the blanks and then forget what we learned. No. God tests our hearts. There will be times when things get hard.

Days when the way seems impossible. Nights when getting to our destiny hurts. We're going to be troubled. We'll hit a wall and be tempted to quit. That's the test.

What do we usually do when we hit a wall? We typically give up. Some of us have traveled for years, ended up four miles from our destiny and then quit. We went all the way through the desert. We invested everything. And then we were disappointed. So we lost hope and threw in the towel. That's not how it's supposed to work.

Florence May Chadwick was a record-holding long-distance swimmer. She was the first woman to swim the English Channel in both directions. In 1952 she attempted to swim twenty-six miles from Catalina Island to the mainland in Southern California. Shrouded in fog and battered by the waves, she struggled for hours. Finally, she could take no more, and she gave up. She was a mile from shore. She couldn't see the shoreline because of the fog. She made it 96 percent of the way and gave up with only 4 percent to go. That's painful. But not as painful as some of our lives.

The wise men responded differently. Yes, it may have looked to them as if they were at a dead end, but for them quitting was not an option. It's reasonable for us to surmise that when they hit a wall, they cried out to God for answers. And look how God led them next: He took them back to His Word. Stuck in Jerusalem, with no idea where to go next, the wise men asked King Herod where the King of the Jews was to be born. Herod turned to the religious leaders of Israel, and they turned to the Scriptures:

Gathering together all the chief priests and scribes of the people, [Herod] inquired of them where the Messiah was to be born. They said to him, "In Bethlehem of Judea; for this is what has been written by the prophet:

'And you, Bethlehem, land of Judah,
Are by no means least among the leaders of Judah;
For out of you shall come forth a Ruler
Who will shepherd My people Israel.'" (Matt. 2:4-6)

The Holy Spirit wrote the Bible. It's the Word of God. So He will speak to us through this Word. We need to read the Bible and then listen for God to speak into our situation. If God really is God, His words to us should blow up our world. If the words in the Bible really are true, they should radically impact our life. When God speaks to us, it changes everything. For the magi this made sense. After all, their journey to Jerusalem had started when they read a prophecy in the Jewish holy writings and then saw a star in the sky. Maybe one of them had received a prophetic word as well. But it all came back to searching the Word and listening for God's voice.

When we hit a wall, we cannot give up. We need to fill the gap. Remember the gap? We saw the gap between God's promise and its fulfillment that the shepherds had to fill. This gap has to be filled by the Word of God and by faith in God. And it's got to be filled by obedience. God gives us a promise, but we've got to get up and do something. This is when transformation comes.

"But Pastor Dan, it hurts! And I'm tired. I thought this would feel better!" It's not going to feel better sometimes. But it is still God. The wise men were four lousy miles away. What if they had gone home?

Look what happened next.

In the Christmas story, the magi weren't the only troubled ones. Their question "Where is the baby?" posed a big problem for King Herod. If a new king had been born, it was a threat to him. After all, where would that leave him? So after helping the wise men figure out where the baby had been born, here's what Herod did:

> Herod secretly called the magi and determined from them the exact time the star appeared. And he sent them to Bethlehem and said, "Go and search carefully for the Child; and when you have found Him, report to me, so that I too may come and worship Him." After hearing the king, they went their way; and the star, which they had seen in the east, went on before them until it came and stood over the place where the Child was. (2:7–9)

Sometimes when God moves supernaturally, only certain people see it. In the Christmas story, not everybody saw the star. The wise men did. It was their GPS. But Herod and his men didn't see it—or they would have followed it themselves.

When did the star reappear? After the wise men cried out to God, heard His voice and obeyed. When they went.

Some of us have made our own journeys from Persia to Jerusalem. We may not have quit and gone home after being disappointed, but we didn't go any further either. We got stuck. We quit the race before we reached our destination.

We all get discouraged. Every one of us. But don't quit. Don't give up hope. God is worth pursuing. We need to get up and go again. Each one of us has a destiny.

Was the pursuit worth it for the magi? Think about it. When they started following the star again, the same thing that had happened to the shepherds also happened to them. The Bible says, "When they saw the star, they rejoiced exceedingly with great joy" (2:10).

What happened when the shepherds obeyed? They rejoiced. What happened when the magi obeyed? They rejoiced.

This is exactly what we should do every time God fulfills His word in us. We should worship Him. We should worship Him because He's worthy of being worshiped. We should worship Him because He is the fulfillment of our destiny. We should worship Him because He fills us with hope and purpose and possibility. We say, "Okay, God met me!" And we rejoice.

We should worship God because He fills us with hope and purpose and possibility.

So after a long and dangerous journey with an unexpected twist at the end, God's word to the wise men was fulfilled! But wait a minute. One more thing. Why in the world did God ask the wise men to give up two years of their lives, get on camels, go all the way across the desert, keep going after they were initially disappointed—all this for one day with a little kid?

The Greek word used to refer to Jesus here is *pattion*, meaning "toddler." Jesus was probably two or three years old by the time the magi found Him. Did they come to see a toddler? No way. They came to see a King. They knew that this little boy was no ordinary child. They believed that this child would change their destiny. The magi saw the child, fell down and worshiped Him. Why? Because He wasn't just a toddler. He was a King.

> After coming into the house they saw the Child with Mary His mother; and they fell to the ground and worshiped Him. Then, opening their treasures, they presented to Him gifts of gold, frankincense, and myrrh. (2:11)

The wise men had carried their treasure through the desert at great risk. Robbers thrived on the route they had taken. But it had been worth the risk. They gladly presented their treasures—gifts of gold, frankincense and myrrh—to Jesus, the King of hope.

Now in our journey there is always a supernatural part and a practical part. The spiritual part in the magi's journey is pretty obvious. The magi presented gifts and bowed down to worship Jesus. They put their treasure before their King and offered Him praise. But what was the practical part? Their King was going to need this treasure.

After the magi gave Jesus their gifts, an angel appeared to them and alerted them not to return to Herod. They were to take an alternate route home, traveling through another country. So off they went.

But the child King was in grave danger:

> Now when [the wise men] had gone, behold, an angel of the Lord appeared to Joseph in a dream and said, "Get up! Take the Child and His mother and flee to Egypt, and remain there until I tell you; for Herod is going to search

for the Child to destroy Him." So Joseph got up and took the Child and His mother while it was still night, and left for Egypt. (2:13–14)

When Herod realized that the magi hadn't returned to Jerusalem with a report on the location of the baby, he grew angry. Where was this new king? He had to be stopped. So Herod put in motion a cruel and terrifying plan: he issued a decree and started killing baby boys two years of age and younger. It was an ugly saga.

Joseph and Mary now had to take Jesus and flee town in the middle of the night. Another test, this time for Mary and Joe. Who would have ever thought that if this was God—and it was—that they would have to run for their lives under the cover of darkness? But they did. God had His purposes for that too. But watch: Joseph and Mary had with them the gifts given them by the wise men, valuable treasures of gold, frankincense and myrrh. Likely work would be difficult for Joseph to find on his way to Egypt. He and his little family would need the money that these gifts would provide. The magi's treasure suddenly became not only spiritual but definitely practical. All along, God knew what His Son would need.

Remember, our journey isn't always going to be easy. Sometimes it will be downright hard! But if we obey, we will hear God speak, and we will see God's hand of destiny all along our way. This is how God works. He knows our need for direction, for provision, for hope—and He always provides. He is the King of hope.

This was the wise men's destiny. It was Joseph and Mary and Jesus' destiny. And it is your destiny as well.

Chapter 5

THE KING OF HOPE IN YOU

God willed to make known what is the riches of the glory of this mystery among the Gentiles, which is Christ in you, the hope of glory.
COLOSSIANS 1:27

You may have noticed that there's no quiz at the beginning of this chapter. Don't be too disappointed—we'll have one later on. This quiz might actually be a bit tougher than the previous ones, though. It will help you evaluate how much you know not so much about the Christmas story but about your own.

If you're anything like me, your life story hasn't gone quite the way you expected it to. Maybe you had great plans for going to college, landing the perfect career, getting married to that gorgeous person, having two and a half kids . . . But somehow you've ended up with a pretty mundane existence. You go to work or you stay home with the kids day after day, but you feel kind of like the shepherds must have—obscure, unnoticed, unimportant. No one even seems to notice you or appreciate you. How did you end up here?

Or maybe you're like the wise men. Long ago you heard God speaking to you, drawing you to embark on some exciting adventure for Him, and you took big risks to seek God, to pursue Him, to go where you believed He was leading you—only to turn up empty. "Maybe I totally missed it, Pastor Dan. I thought God was leading me here, but now I'm really not sure what to think." You're tired, not to mention confused. You wonder if you should just quit and go home.

Maybe you were living a nice, quiet life, happily going about your own business, when suddenly God came along and blew up your world the way He did Mary and Joseph's. Now you're facing a tough dilemma: Your family and friends totally won't get what God is asking you to do. They might even reject you completely if you do what God is asking of you. Obeying God will rip you away from everything that feels comfortable and safe to you. But deep inside something tells you that it will be worth it. Will you do it?

Life sure has a way of being unpredictable, doesn't it? I've had my share of unexpected turns in the road. But when God's the One who rocks our boat, we can trust that He is up to something good.

That was true for Mary and Joseph. Sure, when an angel told each of them that Mary would give birth to the King of the universe, it created some ripples in their world, but when they saw the shepherds filing in to worship the baby Jesus as He lay in a manger, they knew that God was up to something great. God left a gap for the shepherds between His word to them and the fulfillment of that word, and the shepherds had to fill the gap with faith and obedience. But when they did, they ended up rejoicing. They were so excited that they told the whole town about what they'd seen. And those guys on camels, the wise guys—they ended up in the wrong city at first, but I'm sure they were glad that they got back on their camels and made it all the way to Bethlehem.

So what was it that made the wise men ride camels for two years? Why did the shepherds leave their sheep and run off to Bethlehem to find a baby lying in a feeding trough? Why did Mary calmly accept God's surprising revelation and Joseph marry his pregnant fiancée even though God's plan completely rearranged their whole world?

Because Jesus is worth it.

Jesus is worth pursuing. The whole reason He came to earth as a baby King is to give us life. He came to lift us out of our hopelessness and our chaos and to fill our lives with possibility and destiny and hope.

But how did Joseph and Mary and the shepherds and the wise men know that their destinies were wrapped up in this King from heaven? What did they understand about Jesus that made them leave their comfort zones and drop everything for Him?

Colossians chapter 1 is a list, a laundry list, of Jesus' greatness. Some people make lists for everything. Well, here's a list of why Jesus is our King. It tells us who Jesus is. It tells us why Mary and Joseph risked their reputations and why the shepherds left their sheep and why the wise guys got on camels and spent two years traveling to see this child who was more than a child.

In verses 13–20 of Colossians chapter 1, Paul gives seven reasons that Jesus is worth pursuing:

Verse 13: He is our deliverer
Verse 14: He is our redeemer
Verse 15: He is our revealer
Verse 16: He is our creator
Verse 17: He is the sustainer

Verse 18: He is our leader

Verse 20: He is our reconciler

These, my friend, are the reasons that the people of the Christ-mas story went looking for Jesus. God obviously gave each of these people supernatural insight into who Jesus was. He gave them understanding into the fact that Jesus was not just a baby but the King of the universe and the King of hope for each of their lives. Let's look at these seven attributes of Jesus and discover how our own hope and destiny, like those of Mary and Joseph and the shepherds and the wise men, are found in Jesus Christ.

First of all, Jesus is our deliverer:

[God] has delivered us from the domain of darkness and transferred us to the kingdom of his beloved Son. (1:13, ESV)

Do you need delivering? We all need some delivering. I sure did when I was bound up by hell. I was living in darkness, and I needed to be saved out of the darkness and brought into the light. Jesus Christ delivers people out of the authority of darkness and into His kingdom of light. The Bible literally says that He transfers us. Maybe you need a transfer from darkness into light. From bondage into life and possibility.

Transfer was a word that the Romans used when they colonized a country that they had conquered. They would transfer a bunch of their own people into that community and take it over and make it Roman. I'll tell you what. I needed a transfer from darkness to light, and Jesus did that for me.

But the good news that Jesus is our deliverer gets even better. Jesus doesn't deliver us just once, when we first come out of darkness and into light. He delivers us even after we become Christians. He delivers us when we get stuck in this world. He delivers us when we get stuck in our circumstances. When we become discouraged, Jesus is our deliverer. Not Fed-Ex or UPS. Jesus.

"Pastor Dan, I don't know where to go from here. I'm stuck!"

Maybe you're stuck right now. "Pastor Dan," you say, "I've tried to obey. I made it to Jerusalem, but I don't know where to go from here. I'm stuck." I've got good news for you: Jesus is still in the business of delivering. Second Corinthians 1:10 says that God "delivered us from so great a death, and does deliver us; in [Him] we trust that he will still deliver us" (NKJV). We ought to be excited about that. I need delivering every single day, and I'm sure you do too. Jesus wants to make us free, and He wants to keep us free. He is in the delivering business.

Here's the second reason that the folks in the Christmas story dropped their lives to pursue Jesus: He is our redeemer. Paul tells us in Colossians 1:14,

In [Jesus] we have redemption, the forgiveness of sins.

Now in Jesus' day the term *redemption* was used in regard to slaves. When a slave was purchased or bought back—in other words, bought out of the marketplace and into new ownership—he or she was referred to as *redeemed*. And Jesus did exactly that for us: He bought us out of sin and into new ownership, paying the price with His own blood. The King of hope was born for that very purpose—to sacrifice His life so that He could buy us out of slavery to sin and give us new life in Him. He bought us with His blood, His life. That's our Christmas gift, you know. Our life.

Do you remember S&H Green Stamps? If you're young, you're saying, "What the heck is an S&H Green Stamp?" We old people remember those, right? "Yeah, and Blue Chip Stamps too, Pastor Dan. They rocked." We'd go to the store, and our mama would buy her groceries and pay the salesperson, and the salesperson would start peeling off Green Stamps for her. When we got home, my mama would set us down at the kitchen table, and we had to lick those things. It was a nightmare. It was like a mild form of child abuse. I'd complain, "Don't we have sponges, Mom? What's up with this?" We had to lick those things and put them in the Green Stamp book or the Blue Chip Stamp book so we could take them to the redemption store. My mama would say, "You lick them, and I'll let you get something."

The King of hope was born for
this very purpose—to sacrifice His life so that
He could buy us out of slavery to sin.

"Mama," I'd gripe, "there ain't nothing in that redemption store that I want." They had toasters and pots and pans. Nothing for kids. But the point is that my mom could buy things with those stamps.

I have some good news. Jesus went to the redemption store, and He saw something there that He thought was worth buying: you and me. And He paid the price for us and for every other person who will allow Him to work in his or her life with the transforming power that only He can bring. He has redeemed us; He has bought us back. We were lost, slaves to sin and far from the purpose that Jesus had made us for. And Jesus gave us life when we didn't have any.

Jesus is our deliver and our redeemer, and now Colossians 1:15 tells us that He is our revealer:

He is the image of the invisible God.

This is such a great picture. The Greek word for *image* is *icon*. It means "an exact representation." Jesus is the image of God, of the Father's heart, and He reveals God to us. If Jesus hadn't come to earth, there is a great deal about the Father that we wouldn't know or understand. John 1:18 says this: "No one has ever seen God. But the Unique one, who is himself God, is near to the Father's heart. He has revealed God to us" (NLT). Jesus is our revealer.

What did Jesus do when He was on earth? He healed people, fed crowds, blessed little children and ushered people into the kingdom of God. Jesus, the exact representation of God, revealed His Father as a God who cares for people and wants them to walk in His plan and purpose for their lives. He is a God who offers hope.

The fourth thing Colossians 1 tells us is that Jesus is our creator. Look at verses 15–16:

> He is . . . the firstborn of all creation. For by Him all things were created, both in the heavens and on earth, visible and invisible, whether thrones or dominions or rulers or authorities—all things have been created through Him and for Him.

This is important. Why? Because Jesus is the creator of life. And that means He is the creator of hope. He creates destiny, and He creates possibility. It is because of Jesus' creative hand in this world and in our lives that we have something to live for.

Jesus created everything by the spoken word. He spoke life, and it came into being. Whatever He said happened. Hebrews 11:3 tells us that "the worlds were prepared by the word of God, so that what is seen was not made out of things which are visible." No one but Jesus can create something out of nothing. But Jesus created, and still creates, by the power of His word. This is a God worth chasing down, isn't He? That's why the shepherds left their sheep and the wise guys got on their camels. God had given them supernatural insight to understand all these things about Jesus.

You know what we create? Trouble. We always create a mess! But Jesus creates life. That is what He does. He created everything. He created you and me. He knows each of us personally, inside and out, top to bottom. He knows every wild and weird thought that we've ever had. And He's still crazy about us. Is that amazing or what? He created us. And He loves us.

Jesus is not only our deliverer, our redeemer, our revealer and the creator of us and of destiny and possibility. These are all great reasons to follow Him, but there's more. Jesus is also our sustainer:

He is before all things, and in Him all things hold together. (Col. 1:17)

Now we're getting into some powerful stuff. Track with me here.

There are times when our lives spin out of control. "Why, God?" we cry out. Sometimes it's because we've been disobedient. We are living our own way, following our own will, doing our own thing in our own world and yes, creating our own mess. We're living outside the heart of God. Disobedience produces chaos. It makes our world come apart and shatter into fragments. We become fractured, mad at the world, mad at our dad and our mom and ourselves. And we wonder, *what's wrong?*

We don't have to hold it all together. In fact, most of us can't keep it together as well as we think we can.

We need to come back to Jesus. We need to surrender to the King. When we do, He will sustain us. It doesn't mean that life won't be hard sometimes. But Jesus is our sustainer. He's the One who holds everything together.

We don't have to hold it all together. In fact, most of us can't keep it together as well as we think we can. "Man, Pastor Dan, I'm working so hard to keep it all together." How about you surrender and let Jesus keep it all together? He is our sustainer. He's the One who can put our chaos to rest and put life back into our circumstances. That is why He is worth leaving everything behind for.

Sometimes our lives are messed up not because we've been disobedient but because God is stirring the pot. He's trying to get us out of our comfortable place and into His purpose for our life. He wants to use us, but we need a perspective shift first. God may be tearing you to pieces right now, and you're saying, "This is really painful, Pastor Dan. I hate my life." But if you are walking with Jesus, what's happening to you is all God. None of it is an accident. It's destiny.

That's what God did with Joseph, back in the Old Testament, when Joseph was sold into slavery and thrown unjustly into prison. It must have seemed to Joseph as if everything was going horribly wrong, but God knew exactly what was going on with him, and He was arranging things in Joseph's life for good. We know that because we find out later that because of his experiences, Joseph was perfectly positioned to become second in command over the entire country of Egypt and to prepare the country for a coming famine. God arranged circumstances so that Joseph could store up food and save thousands of lives in the famine that followed—including the lives of his own family members. Many years later, after Joseph was finally restored to his family, he told his brothers, "You meant evil against me, but God meant it for good in order to bring about this present result, to preserve many people alive" (Gen. 50:20).

When our world is messed up, whether it's because of our disobedience or because God is stirring up our nest, we need to grasp the reality that Jesus is our sustainer. He sustains us in our chaos.

How does He do it? By His word. We've got to understand this. We just saw that Jesus creates by the spoken word. He also sustains our lives through the spoken word. The Bible is very clear about this. Jesus speaks life, and what He says comes to pass. He also sustains life, and He sustains us, by His spoken word. It says in Matthew 24:35, "Heaven and earth will pass away, but My words will not pass away."

When our world is in chaos, what do we need to do? We talked about this in the previous chapter. We need to get in the Word of God. The written word. We need to get in our Bibles and believe that the Holy Spirit who wrote the written word will speak to us a living word through it. That He will give us a life-sustaining personal word, a *rhema* word, from the Scriptures. We need to get our Bible, get on our face, and say, "God, I need a word from You. My marriage is a wreck, my heart is a mess, my job is jacked up. I don't like the world I'm living in."

God already knows about the mess in our lives. But He's waiting for us to come and talk to Him about it. When we get into the Word and bow down before God and listen for His voice, He will speak to us. We simply need to ask Him for a word. Just one word. When God speaks into our circumstances, everything will change.

Many of us quit, often right before our breakthrough. We have no faith, no hope—and we give up. We go a thousand miles, and then we can't take the disappointment, the heartache, the opposition anymore. We may be only four miles from our breakthrough, but we quit, not realizing that our release is just around the corner. And we get mad at God. What are we thinking? We need to come to Jesus and bow down before Him and ask Him to speak a *rhema* word into our marriage, our kids, our job, our depression.

God is crazy about us. If we ask Him, He will come to us and speak to us. "You will seek Me and find Me when you search for Me with all your heart" (Jer. 29:13).

Why does the process of fulfilling our destiny have to be so painful? Listen to what John the Baptist said: "He must increase, but I must decrease" (John 3:30). God is using our circumstances to get us to die to ourselves so that He can be born in us more deeply. It's painful, it's hard to figure out sometimes, but it's all God. And when He's done with what He's trying to accomplish in us and through us, we'll look back and say, "Wow, I wanted out so badly, but I'm so glad I stayed in."

God is using our circumstances
to get us to die to ourselves
so that He can be born in us more deeply.

God is trying to birth hope in us that we can't get anywhere else. He's trying to do something deep and supernatural in us, and we cannot fulfill our destiny at Nordstrom's or in the refrigerator or in bed with a girlfriend or on drugs with a partner. We can only get it from the King of hope.

Go after God. Go after God! He will show up.

Now watch this sixth one. This one is the toughest. "Pastor Dan, I knew this was going to happen." Yes, this one is hard. But Jesus is worth it.

Now I told you there would be another quiz, right? You'll get to do the quiz in this one. "I don't want another quiz, Pastor Dan. I already flunked one of the others."

Well, you know what's so great about God? We can't ever flunk with God. We get a big F, and He looks at us and says, "It's okay, let's do it again." Guess what else is great about God? When we start the test again, He says, "Let me help you with it this time." I love teachers like that. This is God, my friend. He will help us through. Will He test us? Yes. But He'll help us.

So here's the tough one:

He is also head of the body, the church; and He is the be-ginning, the firstborn from the dead, so that He Himself will come to have first place in everything. (Col. 1:18)

Jesus is our leader. He is the head of the church. He is the be-ginning, and He is the end. This is the Alpha and Omega thing. Jesus is to have first place in everything. He is the firstborn of cre-ation and the firstborn from the dead. Clearly, first place is Jesus' place, not mine or yours. Uh-oh.

We ought to underline that word *everything* in our Bibles. "But Pastor Dan, I don't want Jesus to have first place in *everything!*" I get that. I know how you feel. We think first place is our place, don't we? We don't ever wake up and say, "Boy, I can't wait to be sixty-third today. I hope that when I get to the grocery store, I'm the last one in line. When I get to the bank to make my deposit, I'll be fine if there are twenty-six cars ahead of me." Do we ever think like that?

What place do we always want? First. But there's a problem with that, because that's the place Jesus wants. Isn't it? And when does He want it? "When it's comfortable for me, Pastor Dan; when I'm feeling good about God, when everything's rolling my way." No. When does Jesus want it? All the time—in everything.

I told you this would be tough, right? This is hard. This is the last four miles right here. Giving everything.

Some of us walk with God, we come to church, we get right up to the place where God starts telling us that He can fix what's broken, that He can deliver us from the place where we're trapped—and then we stop. With only four miles to go.

"Pastor Dan, the idea of completely surrendering to God freaks me out." I hear this from people all the time. It's the last four miles, friend. It's our destiny. God wants to be in our business at the deepest level. But that's what scares us. We don't want to let Him in.

Do we really think that God doesn't know how we feel? Why do we think He had to tell us that Jesus wants first place in everything? It's because we try to take first place for ourselves. But God doesn't want to be second or third. We think that if God used to be ninety-ninth in our life and now He's all the way up to number two, we're doing pretty well. No. We're still flunking. Number two is not His place. And this didn't start in the book of Colossians. This started all the way back in the Old Testament.

In Exodus 13, God told Moses that He always wants the first: "Sanctify to Me every firstborn, the first offspring of every womb among the sons of Israel, both of man and beast; it belongs to me" (13:2).

We don't understand this command to Moses very well because we are so separated from the culture of the people in the Old Testament. Most of the folks in Moses' day were ranchers or shepherds. They worked with livestock and agriculture and produce, so when God told them, "I want the firstborn of man and beast," He was literally trying to tell them, "I want the first of all you own."

Say you have two cows—a cow and a steer. And then you get a little baby cow, and you're excited, because now you have three cows. And if your first two cows have more babies, you'll have four or five cows, and you're getting happy, because you make your living from your cows.

So you have that first little cow, and God says to you, "By the way, that's Mine. Hello? That one's Mine."

"No, thank You, God," you say. "Really, actually, that's my cow. I've been waiting a long time for that little calf to pop out of there."

What does God want you to understand? "No, actually, that little cow is the first one. That one's Mine."

Why does God do this? Why does He want us to give Him the first of what we have? Because He wants us to live by faith. "You give Me that one," He says, "you put Me first in everything, and watch Me give you back more than you could ever have imagined."

Remember Jericho? The Israelites marched around the walls of this Canaanite city for seven days in obedience to God, and the walls fell with a huge crash. Before they defeated the city, what did God tell the people to do when they went in? "Don't touch anything. It all belongs to Me" (see Josh. 6:17-19). Why did God say that? Because Jericho was the first city that the Israelites conquered when they came into the promised land. God told them, "This one belongs to Me. You can have the spoil from the rest of the cities, but this one is Mine." God wants to be first in everything.

Sometimes when we're faced with giving God the first, we don't feel much like rejoicing. We think that God doesn't get human nature, that He has no idea how hard surrender is for us. But God knows it's hard. And Jesus knows it's hard, because He went through it too! That's why He gave us encouragement in Matthew 6:33: "Seek first His kingdom and His righteousness, and all these things [food, drink, clothing] will be added to you."

Seek first Him. Seek first Him.

Sixteen times in the Bible God tells us, "I want the firstborn." Sixteen times. Is that enough or not? Why would God say it over and over? Because He's trying to convince us of something.

So in light of that, finally, here's the big pop quiz. It's only a one-question quiz. Are you ready?

Here it is, the million-dollar question: do you want God to be first in your life?

"Really, that's it? That's the quiz? I though you said this was going to be hard! Yes, Pastor Dan, of course I want God to be first in my life."

Most of us probably really do want God to be first. And answering that question may be easy. But actually letting God be first can be a battle. It's a struggle for us to move over and let Him take first place. That's why Jesus put in the Bible a measuring tool so that we can tell if He's really first in our lives or not.

Here it is, the million-dollar question:
do you want God to be first in your life?

Now don't get mad at me. Don't be sending me e-mails after you read this. I'm just telling you what Jesus said. If you get mad, talk to God about it. Here it is. This is how Jesus said that we can measure whether or not God is first in our life: "Where your treasure is, there your heart is first."

Where your treasure is. Listen to the passage:

> Do not store up for yourselves treasures on earth, where moth and rust destroy, and where thieves break in and steal. But store up for yourselves treasures in heaven, where neither moth nor rust destroys, and where thieves do not break in or steal; for where your treasure is, there your heart will be also. (Matt. 6:19–21)

How do we find out whether God is really first in our lives? Two ways: we check our calendar, and we check our checkbook.

First of all, how do we start our day?

"Pastor Dan, I get up at four in the morning. I'm on the road by four thirty. I've got to be at work."

Who's first?

"You're telling me that you think I oughta get up at three thirty or three forty-five and spend time with the Lord before I go to work?"

I'm just asking the question. Who's first? How do we start our day? To whom do we give our time first? That's an incredibly important question.

Second, whom do we write our first check to every month?

"Well, Pastor Dan, I pay for the mortgage and buy groceries for the kids and pay down the MasterCard and the Visa."

Really? Our first check of the month should go to Jesus. That's what the Bible teaches. It's not my idea. I just read it in the Bible. God wants to be first in what? In everything.

God does not tell us these things for the sake of our survival. No. He tells us these things for the sake of our success. God is about our success. He wants to be first in our lives, because if He's first, everything else will work. If He's not first, nothing will work as it should. We will plow the ground over and over, and it will get harder and harder. But if we put Jesus first, we'll rejoice in what He does in our lives, just as the shepherds and the wise men rejoiced when they saw the baby Jesus.

So there was the quiz. *Did you pass?*

Maybe you're not so happy right about now. "This was a good message until you got to this part, Pastor Dan."

Well, let's finish with some good news, because we all flunk this test sometimes, don't we? Putting God first is a struggle for us. But God is so good. He knows that this is hard for us. That's why He put this last reason for following Jesus in the list in Colossians 1.

It says in Colossians 1:20 that Jesus is our reconciler. Not only is He our deliverer, our redeemer, our revealer, our creator, our sustainer and our leader, but Jesus is our reconciler. That means that when there's a breach between us and Him—when we fail—Jesus takes care of it:

> For it was the Father's good pleasure for all the fullness to dwell in Him, and through Him to reconcile all things to Himself, having made peace through the blood of His cross; through Him, I say, whether things on earth or things in heaven. And although you were formerly alienated and hostile in mind, engaged in evil deeds, yet He has now reconciled you in His fleshly body through death, in order to present you before Him holy and blameless and beyond

reproach—if indeed you continue in the faith firmly established and steadfast, and not moved away from the hope of the gospel. (1:19–23)

It always comes back to hope, doesn't it? The message of Jesus is a message of hope. The hope of the gospel.

Let me say this about God. When we fail, He never does! Aren't you glad? He doesn't quit on us when we want to quit on Him at the last four miles and say, "I'm out!" He comes to us and says, "Come on now, get back on that camel; don't worry about your sheep; trust Me with your reputation. Go ahead. I'll help you. I'll do it. I'll even lick your stamps for you." He'll do it all. Isn't this Jesus? Isn't this what He does? This is how He works.

But we first need to get on our camel. We need to go right away looking for Him. We need to leave the misunderstandings of our family and friends in His hands. When we take steps of obedience toward God, He helps us.

Jesus is our reconciler. There's a breach between us and God. Romans 5 talks about it. God created us and destined us for His own purposes, but we turned away from Him. We created a breach with our disobedience and our fear and our discouragement. We need to be reconciled to God. The word *reconciled* literally means "to be brought home." God wants us to bring us back into the destiny He intended us to fulfill when we were born. To give us back the life we lost. To take two estranged parties—Him and us—and bring us back together. Romans 5:6–11 says this:

When we were utterly helpless, Christ came at just the right time and died for us sinners. Now, most people would not be willing to die for an upright person, though someone might perhaps be willing to die for a person who is especially good. But God showed his great love for us by sending Christ to die for us while we were still sinners. And since we have been made right in God's sight by the blood of Christ, he will certainly save us from God's condemnation. For since our friendship with God was restored by the death of his Son while we were still his enemies, we will certainly be saved through the life of his Son. So now we can rejoice. (NLT)

We can rejoice in this wonderful new relationship that we have with God, because our Lord Jesus Christ has made us friends of God.

Remember, the Christmas story is not about a baby. It is about a King—the King of hope. Joseph and Mary and the shepherds and the wise men figured this out. They understood somehow by God's revelation that Jesus is our deliverer, our redeemer, our revealer, our creator, our sustainer, our leader and our reconciler. God has given us in Jesus Christ exactly what we need. And what we need is hope.

Further down in Colossians chapter 1, Paul tells us what this hope is:

Of this church I was made a minister according to the stewardship from God bestowed on me for your benefit, so that I might fully carry out the preaching of the word of God, that is, the mystery which has been hidden from the past ages and generations, but has now been manifested to His saints, to whom God willed to make known what is the riches of the glory of this mystery among the Gentiles, which is Christ in you, the hope of glory. (1:25-27)

God has manifested a mystery to the saints—to those of us who trust God: the gospel is actually Christ in us, the hope of glory. Christ inside us, our hope.

Remember, the Christmas story is not about a baby. It is about a King—the King of hope.

What does it look like when the King of hope lives inside us?

Jimmy Shipman was one of my best friends. He and I used to play ball together. He was a hardcore African American gangster kind of guy from Los Angeles, and he got saved. I used to tease him about his pictures from when he was young—he looked like one of the Temptations with his gigantic afro. Several years ago, Jimmy got sick with leukemia. He fought it for years, but one day his daughter called me and said, "Pastor Dan, come to the hospital fast. Dad's really sick." I got there as fast as I could. As soon as I saw Jimmy, he said to me, "Pastor Dan, I'm really sorry that I'm not feeling well today." He apologized to me for not feeling well! Jimmy died just twenty minutes later.

How could a person in such circumstances be more concerned with another person than with himself? He could do it because God was in him. Because Christ, the hope of glory, was in him. Jimmy had settled every issue in his life. He had completely and totally surrendered to the King of hope. And when God pulled his ticket, he was good to go.

127

When it comes to my own story, I'm so glad I made it to where I am. There were so many times when I told God, "I'm done; I'm out! I hate my life, I hate my world, I don't want the job!" But I stayed in. And I'm so glad I did.

What about you? What does "Christ in you" mean for your story?

Maybe it means that when your family and friends misunderstand you, you hold on to what God has told you, leaving your reputation in God's hands and trusting Him to speak to your loved ones. Or when you feel lonely and unappreciated, you keep working, doing your best, knowing that God sees you and knows your address and will fulfill His promise to you. Or when you've tried to obey, but nothing makes sense anymore, and you're tired and confused and you wonder if you've totally missed God's voice, you get in the Word and listen for God's *rhema* word to you—and then you go the last four miles.

That's what hope is, friend. We have a confident hope reserved in heaven for us, and when we know that, we can relax. We can trust God with our past, our present and our future. Our story becomes God's story worked out in the details of our lives.

The hope that Jesus came to give us can never be taken from us by any person or any circumstance. Remember what the Bible says: "If God is for us, who is against us?" (Rom. 8:31). The answer is nobody. Neither death nor life nor angels nor principalities can separate us from the love of God in Christ Jesus. No circumstance, no situation. If we say yes to God and stay in—don't give in, don't get out—God will do a great and supernatural work inside us.

Christ in us, the hope of glory. Not Christ out there in the world, in our refrigerator, at the shopping mall, in a new car. Those things can never be our hope. Jesus Christ in us is our hope. When we let God have His way with our heart, it's true—He'll tear us to pieces.

He'll bring us to the point of death, turn us inside out. But it's because He loves us so much. Afterward He'll birth Himself in us in such a deep, supernatural way that we will look up and realize that we are not the same people we used to be. Now we are people of destiny. Full of the glory of God and the power of the Spirit. This is how God works.

This is the Christmas story.

If you don't know Jesus Christ, I want to tell you that He knows you. He created you. You need not walk away from this story without Him. Come to Him. Jesus wants to sustain you and redeem you and reconcile you. God is talking to you, but you've got to come. Fill the gap in your life with faith in Jesus Christ. Bow your heart before the King of hope, and tell Him how much you need Him. Tell Him that you don't understand Him completely but that you do believe He died so that you could live. Tell Him that you are ready to surrender to His will and to His way today. Pray with me, won't you?

Father, thank You for Christmas. Thank You for the hope that is all over the Christmas story. Thank You that didn't abandon us when our lives were a mess and we didn't understand our destiny. We might walk away from You, but You will never walk away from us. You come to us and say, "Just four more miles. Trust Me. Come on." Lord, so many people have given up hope. Will You restore hope to each one? Will You speak life back into us with Your still, small voice, with Your rhema *word that redeems us, restores us, reconciles us, sustains us? Speak supernaturally to people's hearts so that they will realize You haven't quit on them, even though their story is hard. We pray in the powerful name of Jesus that in the story of Christmas and in the story of their own lives people will see You, the King of hope. Amen.*

ABOUT THE AUTHOR

○ ○ ○

Dan Carroll grew up in Pomona, California. In February of 1970, he received Christ as his Savior at a Youth for Christ meeting. In 1976 he received a B.A. in Religion from the University of La Verne. In 1979 he received his M.A. in Education from the Claremont Graduate University, and he received an M.A. in Christian Ministry from the International School of Theology in 1987. Pastor Dan completed a Doctorate of Ministry from The King's Seminary in 2004, where he has served on the board with Dr. Jack Hayford for the last twelve years.

In 1987 Pastor Dan began teaching a men's Bible study. For three years the study grew in scope and depth, and the families of the men involved began to come together as well for fellowship. In 1989 Dan and his family went to the Youth With a Mission training school in Kona, Hawaii. They were introduced to cross-cultural ministry in Penang, Malaysia, where Dan received a vision for the world.

After returning to the United States in 1990, Dan was encouraged by the men of his Bible study and their families to plant a church. This became Water of Life Community Church, a church with a weekly attendance today of nearly seven thousand people. He continues today as the senior pastor at Water of Life.

Dan and Gale have been married for thirty-five years and have two adult children, Shane and Katie.

ABOUT WATER OF LIFE

O O O

Water of Life Community Church is a non-denominational evangelical charismatic church. This means that we are devoted to studying and obeying the Bible, which is the Word of God, and we believe in the baptism of the Holy Spirit and the modern-day operation of the gifts proclaimed in the New Testament.

Water of Life was established on Sunday, October 28, 1990, when a group of twenty-one adults and eleven children gathered together to worship at the La Petite Childcare building in Rancho Cucamonga, California. It was a fellowship that arose from a men's Bible study, a group of people who grew together, and a body that is now committed together to seek God's plan as a church family.

Many people love God but have become disillusioned with the church. Therefore, a church that offers a personal encounter with Jesus Christ and growth in His Word without the clutter of an overly structured environment has great appeal. Because we want to maintain the integrity and purity of our spiritual purpose, we do not have a rigorous structure with multitudes of committees or membership requirements.

Our desire is to walk by faith and in deep trust of our Lord. Consequently, you will not see us take an offering. Rather, we believe that the giving of tithes and offerings is worship to Jesus Christ and an expression of the relationship between each individual giver and the Lord.

Although Water of Life is a non-denominational church, we consider ourselves a church that is interdependent with the rest of the body of Christ. Our church is governed by our pastors and our elder board. Additionally, our senior pastor is accountable to an outside group of senior pastors from other local churches as well as to an internationally recognized leader from the Four-square denomination.

○ ○ ○

OUR CORE VALUES

○ ○ ○

Healing

Healing is the very starting point of a transformed life. It speaks to maturing people into a closer relationship with Christ, not just to getting better inside. Jesus put a huge value on healing—putting people back together again. Healing of sick, wounded and broken lives is a high priority to a compassionate and loving God:

> The Spirit of the LORD is upon me, for he has anointed me to bring Good News to the poor. He has sent me to proclaim that captives will be released, that the blind will see, that the oppressed will be set free, and that the time of the LORD's favor has come (Luke 4:18–19, NLT).

Healing is so important to God that He made it a key part of discipleship, or growing in Jesus. Healing occurred many times in Jesus' ministry, and miracles frequently occurred. But Jesus' healing was not just about making people well physically. Rather, it was to restore them in the kingdom of God, to bring them into a right relationship with God. Ephesians 4:11–13 talks of apostles, prophets, evangelists, pastors and teachers all having the responsibility "to equip God's people to do his work and build up the church, the body of Christ . . . until we all come to such unity in our faith and knowledge of God's Son that we will be mature in the Lord, measuring up to the full and complete standard of Christ" (NLT). The word *equip*, *kartatizo* in Greek, means "to mend, restore and be put back together."

> I will sprinkle clean water on you, and you will be clean. Your filth will be washed away, and you will no longer worship idols. And I will give you a new heart, and I will put a new spirit in you. I will take out your stony, stubborn heart and give you a tender, responsive heart. And I will put my Spirit in you so you will follow my decrees and be careful to obey my regulations. (Ezek. 36:25–27, NLT)

The goal in all we do must be transformation—that is where winning begins. God has called us into relationship with one another so that we can be healed and then become instruments of His healing.

> Blessed be the God and Father of our Lord Jesus Christ, the Father of mercies and God of all comfort, who comforts us in all our affliction so that we will be able to comfort those who are in any affliction with the comfort with which we ourselves are comforted by God (2 Cor. 1:3-4).

God does not call us to store up what He gives us but to pass it on to others. Transformation occurs in our church's small groups as well as in our healing and recovery groups, in which people can find support, care, prayer and encouragement.

Sending

Sending is our second core value. We believe it is foundational to all that God wants to do in us.

Everything about us likes to be comfortable, *but Jesus told us that the way for us to grow is to be stretched out* (*ekteno* in the Greek). We need to get out of our comfort zones.

In Acts 13:1–3 we read that the church in Jerusalem sent Paul and Barnabas out on the first real missionary journey. Their goal was to reproduce the work God had done in them and in other believers by spreading the word of Jesus' love and transforming lives and starting churches. This church-planting model has been followed in various forms ever since. Our desire at Water of Life is to send teams out for short-term exposure on a regular basis and at the same time to train and expose our church to as many cross-cultural types of ministry as possible. This includes those near to us (in our valley) and those far from us (all over the world). In our history we have sent short-term teams to between fifteen and twenty different countries, including Malaysia, Hong Kong, Russia, China, Jamaica, Venezuela, Guatemala, Lebanon, Panama, Kenya, Nicaragua, El Salvador, Cuba and Honduras. More recently, we have sent teams to Mexico, Cambodia and Thailand.

Jesus told His disciples in Matthew 28:19, "Go therefore and make disciples of all the nations, baptizing them in the name of the Father and the Son and the Holy Spirit." In Acts 1:4–8 He told them more:

> Gathering them together, He commanded them not to leave Jerusalem, but to wait for what the Father had promised, "Which," He said, "you heard of from Me; for John

baptized with water, but you will be baptized with the Holy Spirit not many days from now." So when they had come together, they were asking Him, saying, "Lord, is it at this time You are restoring the kingdom to Israel?" He said to them, "It is not for you to know times or epochs which the Father has fixed by His own authority; but you will receive power when the Holy Spirit has come upon you; and you shall be My witnesses both in Jerusalem, and in all Judea and Samaria, and even to the remotest part of the earth.

Jerusalem and Judea were home to Jesus and the disciples—that is, local. So we likewise do local outreach at our food-and-clothing warehouse, at Adopt-a-Block, at Mobile Medical Unit and with our annual Trunk-or-Treat Halloween-alternative event. The remote parts of the world for Water of Life are Cambodia and Thailand as well as other nations we have reached. This outreach is all based on Holy Spirit empowerment, and we seek to establish long-term relationships in each of these areas. This will result in transformed lives—in us as we go and in others as they receive.

Equipping

And He gave some as apostles, and some as prophets, and some as evangelists, and some as pastors and teachers, for the equipping of the saints for the work of service, to the building up of the body of Christ. (Eph. 4:11–12)

This core value, like the ones before it, speaks to transforming lives. At Water of Life *winning* is defined as "a transformed life demonstrated by a person being given to God and given to other people." In regard to equipping, as we at Water of Life learn the truth in the Word of God, we receive training along with it as to what we are to do with what we learn. Following God is not just about words—it is an action. A changed person is one who loves God and loves people as well as serves God and serves people.

Equipping at Water of Life means more than just attending church or a Bible study: "The things which you have heard from me in the presence of many witnesses, entrust these to faithful men who will be able to teach others also" (2 Tim. 2:2).

At Water of Life, equipping means teaching and releasing people with the purpose of both mind transformation and heart transformation. Practically speaking, all our small groups will teach and do outreach ministry in which they extend themselves to others. Individuals as well are provided with the opportunity to serve by caring for others—putting their knowledge to work to give life to other people.

Caring

What use is it, my brethren, if someone says he has faith but has no works? Can that faith save him? If a brother or sister is without clothing and in need of daily food, and one of you says to them, "Go in peace, be warmed and be filled," and yet you do not give them what is necessary for their body, what use is that? Even so faith, if it has no works, is dead, being by itself. (James 2:14–17)

We believe that one of Water of Life's main priorities is to care for those in need. The principle is this: we get so we can give.

We believe this is a part of God's heart for all people. We need the poor and downtrodden as much as they need us. It is through them that we gain the heart of God and the Holy Spirit is able to soften us and impart the Father's heart to us.

The Bible is emphatic about the church's responsibility to care for those in need: "But whoever has the world's goods, and sees his brother [or sister] in need and closes his heart against him, how does the love of God abide in him?" (1 John 3:17).

In Matthew 25 we read that Jesus expects nothing less from His church, which is why this core value is so important at Water of Life.

This expectation is clearly shown in Scripture:

Then the King will say to those on His right, "Come, you who are blessed of My Father, inherit the kingdom prepared for you from the foundation of the world. For I was hungry, and you gave Me something to eat; I was thirsty, and you gave Me something to drink; I was a stranger, and you invited Me in; naked, and you clothed Me; I was sick, and you visited Me; I was in prison, and you came to Me." (Matt. 25:34–36)

We want to be counted among the faithful described above as those who fed the hungry, gave drink to the thirsty, invited the stranger in, clothed the naked, cared for the sick and also visited those in prison. "The King will answer and say to them, 'Truly I say to you, to the extent that you did it to one of these brothers of Mine, even the least of them, you did it to Me" (Matt. 25:40).

Relationships

Lives are transformed through relationships—community and family relationships: "You are citizens along with all of God's holy people. You are members of God's family. . . . We [who believe] are carefully joined together in him, becoming a holy temple for the Lord" (Eph. 2:19, 21, NLT).

Everyone who believes in Jesus is part of His family. He has joined us together, and He tells us that we should get along. He is the One who holds everything together. He holds the world together, He holds marriages together, He holds the church family together and He holds personal relationships together: "He is before all things, and in Him all things hold together" (Col. 1:17).

First Corinthians is quite clear in telling us that He put all of us together; we are one body, and we are supposed to live like we are:

> For even as the body is one and yet has many members, and all the members of the body, though they are many, are one body, so also is Christ. For by one Spirit we were all baptized into one body, whether Jews or Greeks, whether slaves or free, and we were all made to drink of one Spirit. (1 Cor. 12:12–13)

The rules of the family of God are clear and simple: we are called to serve one another. This is only possible through our relationship with Jesus. To have a powerful and on-fire relationship with Jesus, we have to get our mind off ourselves and choose to focus on other people. Christ always did this. He built His relationships with many people based on compassion, and He asks us to do the same. In Mark 1:41, as Jesus spoke with a leper, He was "moved with compassion." He stretched out His hand, touched the leper and healed him. In order for us to be really connected with others at a deep level, we must be compassionate.

The heart of a servant is a heart of compassion. There is power in serving others, and there is also blessing in serving others. As we come together in right relationship with other people, we position ourselves to be blessed by God.

Contact us at:

Water of Life Community Church
7625 East Avenue, Fontana, CA, 92336

Water of Life Administration Office
14418 Miller Avenue, Suite K, Fontana, CA 92336

Phone: 909.463.0103
Fax: 909.463.1436
E-mail: info@wateroflifecc.org